FORGOTTEN FRANCISCANS

TIPVS EORVM QVE FRATRES FACIVNT IN OVO INDIARVM ORBE QVA DICTVM EST OLA TABERIS
AD ORIENTEM OCCIDENTEM SEPTENTRIONEM AC MERIDIEM ET POCVSTOS SVVS ET
TVORVM

PVELLA   PVERI

CANTORES

P.PETRVS DE GATE   MORTVVS

DISCVNT OMNIA   CREATIO PVERI

DISCVNT DOCTRINA   EXAMEN MATRIMON

DISCVNT PENITENTIA   SCRIBVNT NOMEN

F.MARTINVS VALENTINVS PRELATVS   S.FRANCISCVS PATER PIORVM

PRIMI SANCTA ROMANE ECLESIE IOVO INDIARVM ORBE PORTATORES

DISCVNT CONFITERI   BAPTISMVS   MATRIMONIVM

CONFESSIONES

MVLIERES

FORGOTTEN FRANCISCANS

Writings from an Inquisitional Theorist, a Heretic,
and an Inquisitional Deputy

Edited and Translated by Martin Austin Nesvig

The Pennsylvania State University Press
University Park, Pennsylvania

Library of Congress Cataloging-in-Publication Data

Forgotten Franciscans : writings from an Inquisitional
theorist, a heretic, and an Inquisitional deputy / edited
and translated by Martin Austin Nesvig.
        p.   cm.—(Latin American originals ; 5)
Includes bibliographical references and index.
Summary: "Examines writings by three early modern
Spanish Franciscans in Mexico. Alfonso de Castro, an
inquisitional theorist, offers a defense of Indian education. Alonso Cabello, convicted of Erasmianism by
the Mexican Inquisition, discusses Christ's humanity
in a Nativity sermon. Diego Muñoz, an inquisitional
deputy, investigates witchcraft in Celaya"—Provided
by publisher.
ISBN 978-0-271-04872-7 (pbk. : alk. paper)
1. Inquisition—Mexico—History—16th century—
Sources.
2. Mexico—Church history—16th century—Sources.
3. Inquisition—Mexico—History—17th century—
Sources.
4. Mexico—Church history—17th century—Sources.
I. Nesvig, Martin Austin, 1968- .
II. Castro, Alfonso de, 1494/5–1558. On whether the
Indians of the New World should be Instructed in
liberal arts and sacred theology.
III. Cabello, Alonso, b. ca. 1555. In nativitati Domini
ad kalendam. English.
IV. Muñoz, Diego, b. ca. 1550. Witness statements in
Celaya about witchcraft.
V. Title.
VI. Series.

BX1740.M6F67 2011
272'.20972—dc22
                                              2010051158

It is the policy of The Pennsylvania State University
Press to use acid-free paper. Publications on uncoated
stock satisfy the minimum requirements of American
National Standard for Information Sciences—
Permanence of Paper for Printed Library Material,
ANSI Z39.48–1992.

CONTENTS

Latin American Originals (LAO) is a series of primary source texts on colonial Latin America. LAO volumes are accessible, affordable editions of texts translated into English—most of them for the very first time, as is the case with LAO 5. The first half-dozen books in the series illuminate aspects of the Spanish conquests during the century from the 1520s to the 1610s.

Taken in the chronological order of their primary texts, LAO 2, *Invading Guatemala*, shows how reading multiple accounts of conquest wars (in this case, Spanish, Nahua, and Maya versions of the Guatemalan conflict of the 1520s) can explode established narratives and suggest a conquest story that is more complicated, disturbing, and revealing. LAO 1, *Invading Colombia*, challenges us to view the difficult Spanish invasion of Colombia in the 1530s as more representative of conquest campaigns than the better-known assaults on the Mexica and Inca empires. LAO 3, *The Conquest on Trial*, features a fictional embassy of indigenous Americans filing a complaint over the conquest in a court in Spain—the Court of Death. That text, the first theatrical examination of the conquest published in Spain, effectively condensed contemporary debates on colonization into one dramatic package. The forthcoming LAO 6, *Gods of the Andes*, presents a 1594 Jesuit account of Inca religion, depicted sympathetically as a precursor to Christianity. LAO 4, *Defending the Conquest*, is a spirited, ill-humored, and polemic apologia for the Spanish Conquest written by a lesser-known veteran conquistador and submitted for publication—without success—in 1613.

The texts presented here in LAO5 cast light on the spiritual conquest and the conflictive cultural world of the Inquisition in sixteenth-century Mexico. *Forgotten Franciscans* gives us three hitherto unpublished documents: a Spanish theologian's 1543 argument in favor of educating indigenous Mexicans; a 1577 sermon on

Christ's birth from a friar twice prosecuted for heresy by the Inquisition in Mexico; and a 1614 report on an investigation into alleged acts of witchcraft from the Inquisition's sole agent—for four decades—in Mexico's remote mountains of Michoacán. This trio of documents illustrates wonderfully the simple fact that not only were there differences of opinion among the Spanish colonists, but even within the Church—within the Inquisition, within the Franciscan order—there were wildly divergent views of the processes of the spiritual conquest of native peoples.

The source texts to LAO volumes are either archival documents—written in Spanish, Portuguese, or indigenous languages such as Nahuatl, Zapotec, and Maya—or rare books published in the colonial period in their original language (Spanish, Portuguese, Italian, Latin). The contributing authors are historians, anthropologists, art historians, and scholars of literature; they have developed a specialized knowledge that allows them to locate, translate, and present these texts in a way that contributes to scholars' understanding of the period, while also making them readable for students and nonspecialists.

Martin Nesvig has developed just such a knowledge, publishing a flurry of books and articles that have made him one of the world's leading scholars of religion in Mexico. He teaches at the University of Miami, where students insist that Nesvig's intellectual energy and passion make him nothing at all like the opinionated and cantankerous inquisitors about whom he writes and lectures. And yet he is surely, like the no-longer-forgotten Franciscans into whom he has breathed new life, one of a kind. One wonders what his subjects—the theorist, the heretic, and the deputy—would have made of Nesvig's own writings.

—Matthew Restall

ILLUSTRATIONS

ACKNOWLEDGMENTS

This project in many ways draws together various strands of other research projects I have undertaken over the years. I was always struck by the vibrant quality of some of these Franciscans who for linguistic or archival reasons were left to the proverbial dustbin. Michael Francis first suggested that I consider developing a book for the Latin American Originals series, and Matthew Restall has been a generous and patient editor in shepherding the project as editor for the series. The anonymous reviewers offered helpful and critical feedback in revising the manuscript.

The translations themselves benefitted greatly from the advice, input, and criticism of friends and colleagues like Carlos Eire, Kimberly Hossain, Tatiana Seijas, and Hugh Thomas (my medievalist colleague down the hall, not to be confused with the Hispanist of the same name). Tatiana Seijas helped me to track down a copy of Castro's manuscript in the Archive of the Indies in Seville.

Some portions of the research for this book were provided by the National Endowment for the Humanities. Any views, findings, or conclusions expressed in this book do not necessarily reflect those of the NEH.

As useful finding aids, especially for looking up lengthy unidentified quotations of medieval theologians and scriptural citations in Latin in Cabello's sermon, I benefitted from several outstanding websites. If medieval theologians could be transported to our world, I have no doubt that they would marvel at the ease with which we can now conduct certain types of searches for unidentified citations, quotations, and authority discussions. One of the best is http://www.newadvent.org/fathers/. In particular, I want to thank the Franciscan Archive at http://www.franciscan-archive.org, which is a wonderful source for anyone interested in Franciscans and their publications, and which offers an outstanding bilingual version of Bonaventure's

Itinerarium mentis in Deum at http://www.franciscan-archive.org/bonaventura/opera/bono5295.html. Other excellent sources that were of great help were the online searchable Vulgate at http://www.drbo.org/lvb/index.htm and the online searchable King James English Bible at http://www.biblicalproportions.com/modules/ol_bible/.

I would like to thank the staff of the Archivo General de la Nación (Mexico) for making it possible to obtain the photocopies of Cabello's sermon and the various depositions and correspondence of Muñoz from the Inquisition section of the archive. I thank the staff of the Archivo General de Indias for allowing access to photocopy the Castro piece.

As in a previous project, David Rumsey of Cartography Associates was generous in allowing images from his map collection to be reproduced here. I gratefully acknowledge his help and the collection at http://www.davidrumsey.com.

And, of course, Patricia Barriga, besides putting up with me, gives me constant in-house advice on language, and so much more.

Unless otherwise noted, all translations in this volume are mine. Any errors, of translation or fact, are mine.

Introduction

In an open-air chapel in central Mexico, in the shadow of Popocate-
petl and Iztaccihuatl volcanoes, a Franciscan friar sprinkled holy
water on a crowd of some two thousand Nahuas and proclaimed
them baptized. None of the Indians understood the Latin pronounce-
ments, though they did understand the one-hour instruction given
to them in Nahuatl prior to the ceremony. There was a long Meso-
american tradition of adopting the gods of victorious tribes and
empires, and proclaiming submission to this new Christian god,
whose flesh they were to eat in symbolic form in a wafer, was not
entirely unusual for them. But they understood little of the concept
of transubstantiation or of the demand of monotheism that this new
submission implied. This was because many of the Franciscans were
pressed for time. For them, steeped in a vision of the world nearing
the end, only friars and those loyal to friars would be saved when the
Apocalypse came. When the Judgment Day did come—and they were
convinced it would be soon—the Indians they had baptized would be
saved from the devil.[1]

This is a familiar narrative and one that was carried out throughout Mexico in the sixteenth century, but it would be stereotyping to
associate it with all Franciscans, or with all Dominicans, Augustinians, or Jesuits. Many Franciscans did not believe in mass baptism,
and the Dominicans, as a whole, opposed it and were even wary of
baptizing Indians at all.

1. For good discussions of this vein of thought, see George Baudot, *Utopia and
History: The First Chroniclers of Mexican Civilization (1520–1569)*, trans. Bernard R.
Ortiz de Montellano and Thelma Ortiz de Montellano (Niwot: University of Colorado
Press, 1995); John Leddy Phelan, *The Millennial Kingdom of the Franciscans in the
New World*, 2nd ed., revised (Berkeley: University of California Press, 1970); and
D. A. Brading, *The First America: The Spanish Monarchy, Creole Patriots, and the
Liberal State, 1492–1867* (Cambridge: Cambridge University Press, 1991).

The papacy conferred considerable privileges on the Franciscans in the New World. Although the Dominicans had been active in the Caribbean for two decades, the Franciscans, in 1524, were the first missionaries dispatched to Mexico. Developing important and lucrative ties with the newly rich conquistador elite and the faction behind Cortés, at whose specific request they had come, the Franciscans quickly became the wealthiest order, with the most dramatic missionary churches and prime real estate in Mexico-Tenochtitlan, and acted as de facto rulers of large indigenous communities.

As described in both colonial and modern histories, the Franciscans in Mexico became known for a variety of things. One was their heavy emphasis on baptizing the Indians, derived, for many of them, from a millenarian recomposition of condemned ideas of Joachim of Fiore. This view was deeply ingrained in the mentality of many of the early Franciscan missionaries, including the founder of the Mexican mission, Martín de Valencia, and the French Franciscan Maturino Gilberti, who was denounced to the Inquisition for his belief (which he shared with the Augustinian cofounder of the University of Mexico, Alonso de la Veracruz) that diocesan clergy were not necessary for the salvation of the Indians.[2]

Likewise, the Franciscans became known for their attempts to establish schools for the indigenous elite, the best-known being the Franciscan college (Colegio de la Santa Cruz) established in Tlatelolco, in the northern part of the Valley of Mexico, in 1536. This mission was an outgrowth of two strands of Franciscan thought. First, in an effort to convert the Indians to Catholicism, the Franciscans immediately began to learn indigenous languages and produce indigenous language books. Second, it was inspired by humanist views of Church reform—a return to basic sources like the Bible and early Church fathers instead of medieval theologians, an emphasis on Latin education, and a belief that among all nations some individuals were destined for the priesthood and higher education in theology. At Tlatelolco, Franciscan friars trained Indian elites in Latin and Spanish

2. Maturino Gilberti, for example, was attacked for having suggested to the Purépecha Indians around Uruapan that only friars and their followers would be saved when the Apocalypse came: AGN, Inquisición (Inq.), vol. 43, exp. 6 and exp. 20. Also see Arthur Ennis, *Fray Alonso de la Vera Cruz, O.S.A. (1507–1584): A Study of His Life and His Contributions to the Religious and Intellectual Affairs of Early Mexico* (Louvain: E. Warny, 1957).

language, humanist philosophy, and theology. Simultaneously, the friars studied Nahuatl, the lingua franca of central Mexico, through which they could investigate Nahua customs, religion, society, and history. The most famous product of this investigation, and the crown jewel of the Franciscan missionary project, was the massive *General History of New Spain* compiled by Bernardino de Sahagún, today known as the Florentine Codex.[3]

A third component of the Franciscan missionary endeavor is less savory. Franciscan worries that Indians would backslide into paganism along with their old customs like human sacrifice led to some of the most notorious events in the so-called spiritual conquest of Mexico, and one of the most shocking destructions of indigenous culture the world has witnessed. The first bishop of Mexico, Franciscan Juan de Zumárraga, destroyed thousands of images and hundreds of pre-Hispanic books and pictographic histories. And in the Yucatán, Franciscan friar missionary Diego de Landa burned hundreds of Maya pictographic works.[4]

These trajectories and narratives about Franciscan thought and activity in Mexico tend, however, to flatten the considerable ideological diversity of the order in the sixteenth and seventeenth centuries. The collection in this volume of documents in translation—a defense of Indian education from 1543, a sermon on the Nativity of Christ from 1577, and investigations into supposed witchcraft in 1614—aims to provide some first-hand depictions of that complexity of ideas as they related to the missionary project in Mexico and the broader ideological trends in the Franciscan order. For example, Erasmus became deeply influential among Franciscans and other intellectuals in Spain, the Low Countries, and Mexico. He had been particularly critical of an array of late medieval practices in Christendom, especially pilgrimages, building of shrines, and the cult of the saints and Mary. In place of these practices Erasmus promoted a stripped-down, interior, and Christocentric spirituality involving greater scrutiny of one's

3. For good general discussions of the Tlatelolco project and Sahagún, see *General History of the Things of New Spain*, 13 vols., trans. Arthur J. O. Anderson and Charles E. Dibble (Santa Fe, N.M.: School of American Research, 1950–1982); José María Kobayashi, *La educación como conquista (empresa franciscana en México)* (Mexico City: El Colegio de México, 1974); Miguel León-Portilla, *Bernardino de Sahagún: Pionero de la antropología* (Mexico City: UNAM, 1999).

4. E.g., see *Proceso inquisitorial del cacique de Tetzcoco, don Carlos Ometochtzin (Chichimecatecotl)* (Mexico City: Biblioteca Enciclopédica del Estado de México, 1980).

own conscience, reading the Bible, and a return to humanist education. Although his ideas found numerous admirers and devotees,
including many Franciscans, there were also many traditionalists who
saw them as heretical and sacrilegious. Likewise, although the millenarian strand of thought was common among Franciscans, hardly
all Franciscans subscribed to it. Many Franciscans viewed Mexico as
an unspoiled religious terrain that would provide innocent Indians as
perfect new catechumens; others viewed Indians with suspicion, seeing them as prone to polygamy and drinking too much pulque.

Many Franciscans who would have been recognized by their con-
temporaries are now largely forgotten by historians. Others, less well
known in their time, are even less remembered. This volume hopes to
add further texture to the prevailing picture of early modern Spanish Franciscans with a range of materials from three Franciscans who
were involved either directly or indirectly with the missionary project in Mexico. All three were connected intimately with the Inquisition. Alfonso de Castro, an influential theologian from Salamanca
who was confessor to kings, actively published on inquisitional law in
the 1530s and 1540s. Alonso Cabello was born in Seville but became a
Franciscan friar in Mexico City in the 1560s. His affinity and admiration for Erasmus and his criticisms of monastic life made him the
object of scrutiny, and he was twice prosecuted for heresy by the
Mexican Inquisition in the 1570s. Diego Muñoz, a semihermit friar
born in Cholula, was a deputy (*comisario*) of the Mexican Inquisition in the remote rural areas of Michoacán for nearly forty years
(1588–1626) and was the Inquisition's sole agent in the mountainous
western area of Michoacán.

Castro wrote a defense of the rights of Indians to become educated
in theology and train for the priesthood. Cabello penned a variety
of philosophical dialogues in which he criticized monasticism, but
here we present his 1577 sermon on the Nativity of Christ. Muñoz
is known today for his chronicle of the Franciscan mission in Michoacán, written around 1585, but here we present some of the details of
his activities as inquisitional deputy when he investigated presumed
witchcraft in Celaya in 1614.

These three friars span a wide chronological range and represent
divergent ideological trends in the Franciscan order in the sixteenth
and seventeenth centuries. Castro was active as an intellectual in
Salamanca during the early decades of the missionary and conversion

project in Mexico. His concerns about the education of the Indians were part of the broad debate about the proper role of Indians in the Church and the relationship between the missionaries and their Indian charges. By the time Cabello delivered his Nativity sermon in 1577, however, the fervor and idealism of the early missionary years had waned. Indian populations had declined horrifically, and the sense of a vibrant, millenarian Church had gone into retreat. The influence of Erasmus held on in Mexico much longer than it did in Spain, and Cabello was squarely in the middle of a fight for the ideological heart of the Mexican Franciscan enterprise just as Sahagún's massive linguistic, ethnographic, and historical project was ordered banned by the Spanish crown. By the time Muñoz walked into the central square of Celaya in October of 1614 to deliver the announcement that the Inquisition was to investigate witchcraft, the Indian population had reached its nadir. The Franciscan mission was still active in Michoacán, but it had fallen on hard times, and even the principal monastery of the province in Valladolid was literally falling down. Muñoz was living in a shadow world in Michoacán, where Indian populations had almost disappeared in the hot lands and where he spent his time meditating on the nature of the soul in remote mountain villages.

Each of the documents presented here offers a window into a unique moment in the development of the Franciscans in the sixteenth and early seventeenth centuries. Castro has been almost entirely forgotten, mostly because his works were not translated out of their original Latin and went into general disuse after the eighteenth century. Cabello was at the center of the controversy over Erasmus on the ground level in Mexico, but his works were never published and were consigned to the files of the Inquisition, where they went largely unnoticed until Marcel Bataillon mentioned them in his history of Spanish Erasmianism. Muñoz penned hundreds of letters and took hundreds of depositions as the Inquisition's deputy, but, like Cabello's material, this has remained as manuscript buried within the hundreds of volumes of material in the Mexican Inquisition's files.

The Inquisitional Theorist

Alfonso de Castro was born in Zamora, Spain, in 1495. We know little of his family. He began his university studies around 1507,

probably at Alcalá, the newly formed university founded on principles of humanism. In 1510, Castro took the Franciscan habit in
Salamanca, where he spent a considerable amount of his illustrious
career. By 1515 he held a chair of theology at Alcalá, and he was subsequently master of theology in the Franciscan house at Salamanca.
He became an intimate of Charles V, who made him his confessor
as well as royal advisor. In 1526 he traveled to Assisi as a delegate to
the Franciscan general chapter meeting and thereafter returned to
Alcalá to resume his university studies from 1528 to 1532. By 1535
he had made Salamanca his permanent home and received a licenci-
ate in theology from the University of Salamanca. In 1545 and 1547
he attended the Council of Trent as Philip II's theologian. In 1551 he
became superior of the Salamanca Franciscan house. He was nomi-
nated to the see of Compostela in 1557 but fell ill and died on February 4, 1558, before having taken possession of the diocese.[5]

Castro, a prolific and wide-ranging writer, was best known for
his sophisticated discussions of the theory and law of the Inquisition and heresy. The Holy Office of the Inquisition was established
in the 1220s, and jurists and theologians had been writing so-called
inquisitional treatises since the fourteenth century. Castro's *Adversus
omnes haereses* (*Against All Heresies*) went through twenty editions between 1534 and 1568, making it the all-time most-printed
inquisitional treatise. *De justa haereticorum punitione* (*On the Just
Punishment of Heretics*), a much more serious treatise, was first
printed in 1547 and solidified his reputation as a formidable theorist.
Castro's style is complex but elegant. Yet even while he defended the
Inquisition and the necessity of the defense of Catholicism against
Lutheranism and other heresies, Castro admired Erasmus and had a
real sympathy for humanism.

The cumulative effect of Castro's intellectual corpus was mixed.
For example, his homilies on various psalms established him as one
of Salamanca's best public preachers. On the other hand, his erudite
discussions of law and heresy cemented his legacy as the only important Franciscan theologian of the sixteenth century to take up juris-
prudence in relation to divine law and theology. Castro also trained
some of the future censors of the Mexican Inquisition, including one

5. For biographical information on Castro, see Teodoro Olarte, "Alfonso de Castro (1495–1558): Su vida, su tiempo y sus ideas filosóficas-jurídicas," Tesis de licenciatura, Universidad Nacional de Costa Rica, 1946.

of the censors called in the trial against Cabello in 1577 in Mexico City. While Castro never set foot in the Americas, he was clearly well versed in the debates about the legitimacy of the Conquest of the Americas. He was a friend of the holder of the prime chair of theology at the University of Salamanca, Francisco de Vitoria, who had lectured on some of the reasons he felt the Conquest of the Americas was unjustified.

The Heretic

Cabello was born around 1555 in Seville and went to Mexico when he was three years old with his father, Marcelino Cabello, and his mother, Doña Hierónima de Alemán. Although we do not know anything about their backgrounds, his mother's honorific *doña* and his father's status as a *licenciado* (a university graduate lawyer) suggest they were well heeled. His father served as *alcalde* (magistrate) of Oaxaca City and Puebla, and during his youth Cabello lived with his father there from approximately 1558 to 1565. The younger Cabello went to Mexico City when he was ten, around 1565, and subsequently professed in the Franciscan order at age thirteen, around 1569. Fray Alonso resided in Franciscan houses in Michoacán, Cholula, and Toluca before returning to Mexico City to study theology.[6]

Cabello's case is today largely forgotten but was clearly something of a *cause célèbre* in the debates of the 1570s over Erasmianism, humanism, monastic vows, and the Franciscans. Cabello was actually tried twice—once in 1573 and again in 1578—and his story reads something like a *pícaro* novel, though the details are not always precise. Cabello was arrested in Cholula in October 1578 after rumors that he had preached a Nativity sermon in the Franciscan friary in 1577 despite being forbidden after his 1573 conviction for heresy from exercising anything but the most menial of duties in the order. After his arrest a search of his cell turned up the manuscript copy of his Nativity sermon, which is reproduced here: "In nativitati domini

6. The 1573 trial is in AGN, Inq., vol. 116, exp. 1; the 1578 trial in AGN, Inq., vol. 88, exp. 1. I have also relied on José Miranda, *El erasmista mexicano: Fray Alonso Cabello* (Mexico City: UNAM, 1958) for general discussions of Cabello's biography and mishaps.

ad Kalendam."[7] This is an extremely rare case of a manuscript version of a sermon in colonial Mexico surviving. Occasionally prominent and lucrative sermons given on the feast days of major saints or on the sanctification of a new saint were published in colonial Mexico. For example, the Dominican friar Francisco de Arévalo, well known as an orator, gave the feast day sermon for Saint Thomas Aquinas on March 6, 1632, in Mexico and copies of the sermon were printed.[8] Likewise, Alfonso de Castro had a collection of his sermons published in Latin in Salamanca in 1568. But manuscript sermons were usually lost and tended only to survive if they were confiscated as part of a trial.

Eventually, after his two trials for heresy and Erasmianism and the reading of prohibited books, Cabello was exiled from Mexico and returned to Spain. We do not know his fate or if he was prosecuted by the Inquisition there. It is clear, however, that despite the efforts of the Inquisition both in Spain and Mexico, as well as the efforts of antihumanist conservatives like Melchor Cano and Inquisitor General Fernando Valdés, Erasmus continued to be popular among certain segments of the Franciscan order well into the second half of the sixteenth century. Cabello fell squarely in the middle of the debate on Erasmus and demonstrates the difficulty of attempting to quash ideas, especially when there were strong supporters of such ideas within corporate entities like the Franciscan order.

The Inquisitional Deputy

Muñoz was born in Cholula around 1550 and spent most of his adult life in rural Michoacán, far from the center of Franciscan political and administrative activities in the Pátzcuaro basin and Valladolid. We do not know who his parents were, though the seventeenth-century chronicler of the Franciscan mission in Michoacán, Alonso de la Rea, says they were "noble and virtuous," which really tells us nothing, because missionary chronicles usually stressed the virtue of members

7. AGN, Inq., vol. 88, exp. 1. The sermon has been transcribed in Martin Austin Nesvig, "El sermón de un erasmista olvidado," *Boletín del Archivo General de la Nación* [México] 6, no. 5 (2004).

8. *Sermón . . . día del Angélico Doctor Sancto Thomás de Aquino siete de março 1632* (Mexico City: n.p., 1632).

of their orders. It is most likely that he was a *criollo* (an American-born Spaniard), since any admixture of Indian or African blood would have disqualified him from taking on higher orders, though exceptions were occasionally made and rules broken.[9]

Muñoz took his vows to the Franciscan order in Tzintzuntzan, probably some time in the 1560s though possibly as late as the early 1570s. During the 1580s, as far we know, he spent most of his time in the Pátzcuaro area and appears to have gathered a good knowledge of local, mostly Purépecha, culture, as well as some facility with the Purépecha language. Around 1585 he completed a chronicle of the Michoacán province of the Franciscans, which was never published in his lifetime.[10] He also became guardian of the Franciscan houses of Pátzcuaro and Querétaro in the 1590s. Eventually he was elected provincial (the highest-ranking official of a province) twice (ca. 1600 and ca. 1610) and was, it seems, the first *criollo* ever to be elected to this office.[11] He presided over the interim chapter meeting of the Franciscan province of Michoacán in Uruapan as provincial in April 1603.[12] Yet for all his activity and success in administration of the Franciscan mission, he appears to have preferred a contemplative and solitary life. He often wrote to his superiors in Mexico City asking to be relieved of his duties.[13]

From the late 1590s through about 1608, after having lived variously in Pátzcuaro and Querétaro, he appears to have resided primarily in the region west of Valladolid in Pátzcuaro, Uruapan, and Tancítaro and was the Inquisition's deputy in the region. By about 1608 he had moved to a small hermitage in Acahuato, which

---

9. See the discussions in Francisco Morales, *Ethnic and Social Background of the Franciscan Friars in Seventeenth Century Mexico* (Washington, D.C.: Academy of American Franciscan History, 1973); and Magnus Lundberg, "El clero indígena en Hispanoamérica: De la legislación a la implementación y práctica eclesiástica," *Estudios de historia novohispana* 38 (2008).

10. Diego Muñoz, *Descripción de la provincia de San Pedro y San Pablo de Michoacán, en las Indias de la Nueva España,* intro. José Ramírez Flores (Guadalajara: Instituto Jalisciense de Antropología e Historia, 1965).

11. See Morales, *Ethnic and Social Background,* 69n69; and AGN, Inq., vol. 292, exp. s/n, fols. 30–32.

12. AGN, Inq., vol. 270, exp. s/n, fols. 125–28.

13. Alonso de la Rea, *Chrónica de la órden de N. Seráphico P.S. Francisco, Prouincia de S. Pedro y S. Pablo de Mechuacán en la Nueua España* (Mexico City: La viuda de Bernardo de Calderón [Paula de Benavides], 1643), fols. 95–98, discusses his life as a hermit and recluse.

would be his mostly permanent home until his death in late 1625 or 1626.[14] His motives for this move are not clear, but it seems that he had a real affinity for solitude. Acahuato is a remote hamlet between Apatzingán in the low-lying *tierra caliente* (hot lands) and the high-altitude region near Tancítaro. During these three decades he sent an impressive amount of material to the Inquisition in Mexico City. Most of this material survives today as depositions that he took in his legal capacity as *comisario* as well as his correspondence with the inquisitors in Mexico City. Among it can be found a wide range of discussions of local customs, "superstitions," spells, cures, incantations, religious attitudes, and shenanigans by the local clergy. Soliciting young women in the confessional seems to have been widespread. Blasphemy was common among the general population.

Because of its comprehensive quality, Inquisition documentation has been used by a wide range of social, cultural, religious, and intellectual historians. The Inquisition operated as a court of law that had jurisdiction primarily over violations of Catholic doctrine, or heresy. Heresy was considered the explicit rejection of some article of faith or doctrinal point as defined by the Church, theologians, or the General Spanish Inquisition. The Inquisition also had jurisdiction over certain types of blasphemy and "propositions" or those statements that were seen as attacks on the Church but which were not heresy strictly speaking. For example, to say that Mary and Joseph had had sexual intercourse in order for Mary to become pregnant was seen as heresy because it rejected the article of faith of the virgin birth of Christ. On the other hand, statements like "Mary Magdalene is a whore" or "the pope is a pedophile" were not specific heresies but could be prosecuted by the Inquisition. The Inquisition also claimed jurisdiction over certain kinds of witchcraft and "superstitions," the solicitation of sexual favors in the confessional by priests (as a

14. For information on Muñoz's whereabouts, see AGN, Inq., vol. 130, exp. 7; vol. 186, exp. 1; vol. 209, exp. 9; vol. 214, exp. 10; vol. 252, exp. s/n; vol. 253, 2a parte, fols. 303, 311, 316, 318; vol. 257, exp. 3; vol. 265, exp. s/n, fols. 6–8; vol. 270, exp. s/n, fols. 125–28; vol. 272, exp. s/n, fols. 486–89, 505–11, 513–18; vol. 277, exp. 5; vol. 278, exp. 2; vol. 281, exp. s/n, fols. 28–31, 468–75; vol. 283, exp. s/n, fols. 104, 145, 148–51, 333–34, 504; vol. 284; vol. 285, exp. s/n, fols. 361–62; vol. 471, exp. 3, exp. 4, exp. 5, exp. 6, exp. 16, exp. 20, exp. 21, exp. 24; vol. 292, exp. s/n, fols. 21, 30–31, 43, 150; vol. 302; vol. 474, exp. s/n, fols. 508–12; vol. 303, exp. s/n, fols. 35–43; vol. 308, exp. s/n, fols. 136–38; vol. 312, exp. s/n, fols. 29–31, 80, 167; vol. 314, exp. 8a; vol. 322; vol. 332, exp. 2, exp. 4, exp. 6; vol. 335, exp. 79; vol. 346, exp. 7; vol. 473, exp. s/n, fols. 185, 191; vol. 475, exp. s/n, fols. 676–81; vol. 510, exp. 87, exp. 89, exp. 90, exp. 92, exp. 99.

violation of the sacrament of confession), and bigamy (as a violation of the sacrament of marriage). Finally, because inquisitional officials were exempt from most civil court litigation, cases like homicide, rape, theft, assault, and other charges brought against them were heard by the Inquisition.[15]

During inquisitional investigations, witnesses could be compelled to appear in court, or they could appear voluntarily. According to inquisitional law, an edict of the faith, which enjoined all the faithful to unburden their consciences if they had committed any heretical acts or knew of any such acts in the community, was read in the main church of a given town. In large cities like Mexico City, Puebla, and Valladolid, this usually occurred annually. But in smaller cities it was less frequent. The Inquisition in Mexico operated on two geographic levels. The inquisitors themselves, who were the judges of the inquisitional court, resided in Mexico City and heard trials there. Throughout the rest of Mexico, local *comisarios* (deputies) were stationed in larger towns.

Comisarios were empowered by the inquisitors to announce the edict of the faith, to conduct interrogations of witnesses, and to arrest suspects. But they were not empowered legally to conduct actual trials. In some cases inquisitors sent orders to a local *comisario* to carry out some kind of sentence. But in general, only inquisitors conducted formal trials and levied sentences and punishments. In the gravest cases, inquisitors could "relax" a convicted heretic to be executed by secular authorities, though the perception of this type of sentence is considerably exaggerated. Sentences such as fines, public whipping and humiliation, galley slavery, and reclusion in a monastery or hospital were more common.

In many rural areas, no *comisario* was present. This meant that in much of rural Mexico, local people had little contact with the Inquisition and its agents. In the case of Michoacán discussed here, Muñoz was the only inquisitional *comisario* from about 1588 until 1626 for an expansive area that included most of the current state of Michoacán as well as the southeast part of Jalisco, the far western portion of Guerrero, and even occasionally the southern part of Guanajuato. There was an inquisitional *comisario* stationed in the

15. For an overview of the jurisdiction of the Inquisition and typologies of crimes, see Martin Austin Nesvig, *Ideology and Inquisition: The World of the Censors in Early Mexico* (New Haven: Yale University Press, 2009).

diocesan capital, Valladolid, but these *comisarios* were known for their spectacular corruption and also tended only to deal with the city population. The implications of this are breathtaking. Many assume that the Inquisition was a highly efficient mechanism of control and social repression. But consider for a moment what modern-day life would be like if in a region roughly the size of the state of Iowa there were only one sheriff. The lawlessness would be legendary. This was the case, at least in terms of inquisitional law and control, in seventeenth-century Michoacán, and Muñoz was clearly fighting a losing and unwinnable battle against the perceived forces of heresy, blasphemy, and impiety.

Muñoz does not appear to have had much career ambition. In many ways he was a kind of idealized Franciscan friar, devoted to a life of contemplation, poverty, and administering to the sick and uneducated. He often complained in his letters of administrative duties and asked to be allowed to return to his hermit-like existence in the mountains near Acahuato. Nor was he much of an active missionary. He left no discussion of intense conversion efforts, and chronicles of the order mention him as a pious, humble man. He remains something of an enigma. Perhaps it is fitting that he has been largely forgotten by historians, and if in posterity he wished to remain anonymous and forgotten, I hope he will excuse the light cast on him in these pages.

The documents that follow expose both deep rifts in Franciscan thought as well as considerable diversity and complexity: admiration for coupled with deep distrust of Erasmianism; idealistic views of Indian education coupled with views of Indians as superstitious and backward. By shining a light on largely forgotten Franciscans of the early modern period, we can reconsider the mythologies and realities of Franciscan thought.

1

The Inquisitional Theorist in Defense of Indian Education

When Alfonso de Castro wrote his discussion on Indian education and intellect in 1543, it came at a time of intense debate over the legitimacy of the Spanish Conquest of the Indies, over the relative humanity and intelligence of the Indians, and over their qualities as catechumens, neophytes, and eventual full members of the Catholic Church. Much of this debate was a continuation of very old debates about conversion, the role of theology and knowledge, and the relationship between the priesthood and the laity in Catholic thought from the early Church through the medieval period.[1]

Catholic thought had traditionally placed a high premium on a hierarchy of knowledge about Scripture and religious mysteries. The Bible is a composite of ancient languages (Hebrew, Aramaic, Greek), and it was left to the considerable talent and style of Jerome to systematize it into one Latin text, known as the Vulgate. This translation served the Catholic Church for centuries as the standard

1. The most accessible overview of the debate is found in Anthony Pagden, *The Fall of Natural Man: The American Indian and the Origins of Comparative Ethnology* (Cambridge: Cambridge University Press, 1982). There is abundant literature on the subject. For an abbreviated listing, see Venancio D. Carro, *La teología y los teólogos-juristas españoles ante la conquista de América*, 2 vols. (Madrid: Talleres Gráficos Marsiego, 1944); Jean Leclercq, *Jean de Paris el l'ecclésiologie du XIIIe siècle* (Paris: J. Vrin, 1942); William Edward Maguire, *John of Torquemada, O.P.: The Antiquity of the Church* (Washington, D.C.: Catholic University of America Press, 1957); James Muldoon, *Canon Law, the Expansion of Europe, and World Order* (Aldershot: Ashgate, 1998); Edmundo O'Gorman, *Idea del descubrimiento de América: Historia de esa interpretación y crítica de sus fundamentos* (Mexico City: Centro de Estudios Filosóficos, 1951); Ignacio Osorio Romero, *La enseñanza del latín a los indios* (Mexico City: UNAM, 1990).

For discussion of Castro and his role in the development of law and legal theory and as trusted confidant to the Crown, see Santiago Castillo, *Alfonso de Castro y el problema de las leyes penales: O la obligatoriedad moral de las leyes humanas* (Salamanca: Universidad de Salamanca, 1941); Marcelino Rodríguez Molinero, *Origen español de la ciencia del derecho penal: Alfonso de Castro y su sistema penal* (Madrid: Cisneros, 1959); Manuel de Castro, "Fr. Alfonso de Castro, O.F.M. (1495–1558), consejero de Carlos V y Felipe II," *Salmanticensis* 6 (1958).

biblical source, though some scholars continued to work in the original languages. Likewise, through the works of scholar-priests of late antiquity like Augustine, the Catholic Church began to formalize the dichotomy of knowledge between priests and laity, with the assumption that priests, trained in Latin, were the holders and gatekeepers of specialized knowledge about the more complex mysteries of the Christian faith, like the metaphysics of the Trinity and the humanity of Christ.

This separation of knowledge meant that for several centuries the Catholic priesthood controlled and regulated spiritual knowledge and formal theology and in turn the teaching of that knowledge both to the laity as well as to aspiring theologians and priests. Challenges to this monopoly of knowledge came in the form of the Waldensians, for example, in the late twelfth and thirteenth centuries, who argued that individuals who were not ordained priests could preach on spiritual and Christian themes. Other heresies, like Catharism in southern France, argued against the monopoly of knowledge by Catholic priests.[2] The response from the Catholic Church was to formalize the Inquisition, which was devised originally in the 1220s as kind of itinerant court and investigation into heresy and often led by Dominican friars from the newly established Order of Preachers, founded by the Castilian Domingo de Guzmán. The Franciscan Order was founded contemporaneously and promoted a kind of radical poverty and spiritualism. Unlike the Waldensians, however, Francis of Assisi accepted the overtures of the papacy to remain within the fold of the Catholic Church.

For the rest of the medieval period, the Catholic Church asserted the knowledge of spiritual mysteries and theology as the exclusive provenance of ordained priests. Attempts to reform this position were met with intransigence, as was the case when John Hus was executed

2. For some discussions of these emergent heresies and the response, in the form of the development of the Inquisition, see Laurent Albaret, ed., *Les Inquisiteurs: Portraits de défenseurs de la foi en Languedoc (XIIIe–XIVe siècles)* (Toulouse: Editions Privat, 2001); Tomás de Bustos, *Santo Domingo de Guzmán: Predicador del Evangelio* (Salamanca: Editorial San Esteban, 2000); Antoine Dondaine, "Le manuel de l'inquisiteur (1230–1330)," *Archivum Fratrum Praedicatorum* 18 (1947); James B. Given, *Inquisition and Medieval Society: Power, Discipline, and Resistance in Languedoc* (Ithaca: Cornell University Press, 1997); Emmanuel LeRoy Ladurie, *Montaillou: The Promised Land of Error*, trans. Barbara Bray (New York: Vintage, 1978); Kenneth Pennington, *Pope and Bishops: The Papal Monarchy in the Twelfth and Thirteenth Centuries* (Philadelphia: University of Pennsylvania Press, 1984).

at the Council of Constance in 1415 for his various attacks on the office of the priesthood.[3] This attempt at reform would then resurface famously with Martin Luther in the 1520s, with the result that the Church was, once and for all, split apart.

Part of the debate on the monopoly of knowledge by the priest class was a debate on the appropriateness of translating the Bible to allow the non-Latinized laity to read Scripture. In the text translated here, Castro inserts his discussion squarely in the middle of this debate. On the one hand, Castro had been a defender of the prohibition of vernacular translations of the Bible. He argued against the vernacular translation of Scripture forcefully in his two main treatises on heresy, *Adversus omnes haereses* and *De justa haereticorum punitione*.[4] But Castro, in this text, goes on to ask a second question: if the Bible was to remain in Latin, who should be instructed in Latin in order to read, interpret, and preach Scripture to the laity? Castro argues that the Indians of the Americas were much like the unconverted or newly converted peoples of the eastern Mediterranean in the first two centuries after Christ: some were inherently intelligent and capable of learning the sacred mysteries of theology, while most were not. Castro's discussion was squarely in the middle of the debate about translating Scripture into vernacular languages. This debate would have results in the Spanish Inquisition's prohibition of vernacular translations of Scripture in 1554. Later, in reaction to the discovery that a Nahuatl translation of Ecclesiastes was circulating in Mexico, the translation of Scripture into Indian languages was specifically banned in 1577. Sahagún had argued against this prohibition and supported an exemption of the rule for Indian languages, but the Dominican censors called in to argue the case supported the ban, which had been effected by the central commission of the Spanish Inquisition in Madrid.[5]

This controversy also took place within the emerging debate about Indians and their place in the Church in the Americas. Many idealistic Franciscans, like Castro, wanted the Indians to become fully integrated members of the Church. In Castro's view, the most intellectually talented Indians should be cultivated for careers in the

3. See John Hine Mundy and Kennerly M. Woody, eds., *The Council of Constance: The Unification of the Church* (New York: Columbia University Press, 1961).
4. See Nesvig, *Ideology and Inquisition,* 57–61.
5. The debate is found in AGN, Inq., vol. 43, exp. 4.

priesthood, theology, and the universities. Others, principally Dominicans but also many Franciscans, bitterly opposed this view. The 1555 and 1565 Councils of the Mexican Church, led by the archbishop of Mexico, Alonso de Montúfar, and his right-hand man, Bartolomé de Ledesma, quashed the plans for an Indian clergy, and Indians were formally forbidden from taking any higher orders in the Church (including the priesthood).[6]

Castro's discussion is centered firmly on the question of the relative intelligence of the Indians and of the appropriateness of instructing new Christians in theology and the higher mysteries of the Christian faith. But this discussion took place within a much broader debate about the Indians that had its most famous and best-known debater in Francisco de Vitoria. While Castro was never a professor in the faculty at the University of Salamanca, he was nevertheless well known in Salamanca both as a popular preacher and as a powerful and respected theologian with ties to the Crown. Vitoria, on the other hand, held the prime chair of theology at the University of Salamanca, from which he delivered lectures on the legality and morality of the Conquest of the Indies, on just war, and on various other topics.[7]

6. Some scholars have tried to whitewash the Dominican opposition to Indian education. It is well known that the founder of the Dominican mission in Mexico, Domingo de Betanzos, viewed the Indians as children who would never intellectually advance, though there seems to be some evidence that his views softened later in life. In particular, Alberto María Carreño in his *Fr. Domingo de Betanzos: Fundador en la Nueva España de la venerable orden dominica* (Mexico City: Imprenta Victoria, 1924) suggests that Betanzos had been unfairly pilloried as an antihumanist (the charge, however, seems all too accurate). For a recent study (quite sympathetic), see Magnus Lundberg, "Unity and Conflict: The Church Politics of Alonso de Montúfar, O.P., Archbishop of Mexico, 1554–1572" (Ph.D. diss., Lund University, 2004). For general discussion, see Kobayashi, *La educación como conquista.* For some discussion of Ledesma, see Ana de Zaballa Beascoechea and Josep-Ignasi Sarayana, "Bartolomé de Ledesma y su doctrina sobre los justos títulos," in *Actas del III Congreso Internacional sobre los Dominicos y el nuevo mundo* (Madrid: Editorial Deimos, 1991). For more extensive discussion of the broader debate about the adaptation of Mexica culture and religion to Spanish Catholicism, see Osvaldo Pardo, *The Origins of Mexican Catholicism: Nahua Rituals and Christian Sacraments in Sixteenth-Century Mexico* (Ann Arbor: University of Michigan Press, 2004).

7. For comprehensive discussion, see Juan Belda Plans, *La escuela de Salamanca y la renovación de la teología en el siglo XVI,* 2 vols. (Madrid: Biblioteca de Autores Cristianos, 2000); and Demetrio Ramos et al., *La ética en la conquista de América: Francisco de Vitoria y la escuela de Salamanca* (Madrid: Consejo Superior de Investigaciones Científicas, 1984).

For five decades, beginning in the 1490s, both in Crown-sponsored debates as well as in university lectures, jurists, theologians, and missionaries had ventilated concerns about the Conquest and the role of the Indians. These debates began at the behest of the Catholic Monarchs, Ferdinand and Isabella, after the establishment of Spanish rule in the Caribbean. The monarchs, concerned that conquistadors would usurp the rights of the Crown over their subjects, commissioned jurists and friars to resolve the issue. The result was the Laws of Burgos in 1512, which asserted that Indians were lawful subjects of the Spanish Crown. While many have derided these as a precursor to imperialist enslavement, in the context of other expanding European powers of the sixteenth, seventeenth, and eighteenth centuries, the Spanish Crown actually extended, in law and in theory, considerable protections to the Indians, including the prohibition of their wholesale enslavement. These laws legalized the system of *encomienda,* in which Indians were entrusted to Spanish overseers who, in exchange for the labor granted to them, were in theory to protect the Indians and aid their conversion to Christianity. The Laws of Burgos, however, could not control the ambition of conquistadors and *encomenderos,* who often flouted them to a horrifying degree.[8]

By the time Cortés conquered Mexico in 1521, the enslavement and abuse of Indians was widespread, despite their legal protections. Bartolomé de las Casas, the *encomendero* turned Dominican friar and missionary, lobbied extensively against the abuse of the Indians. Other missionaries and friars added horrific eyewitness details of the rape, enslavement, murder, and destruction of the Indians. Of course, many such accounts were exaggerated for effect. But there was a real and substantive debate among missionaries about the morality of the *encomienda* system. In theory Indian slavery was formally forbidden in 1542 with the New Laws, which also indicated the *encomiendas* would henceforth not be inheritable.

While this debate was taking place, there were simultaneous debates about the legal and theological implications of the Conquest. Vitoria argued that the Indians of the New World possessed full dominion as societies and could not be despoiled of this dominion through simple fiat. Much of the Conquest was in fact illegal, he maintained, because it was based on Pope Alexander's 'donation'

---

8. For discussion and trajectory of these specific debates on the Laws of Burgos and Las Casas, see Pagden, *Fall of Natural Man.*

of the Americas to the Spanish Crown in 1493, in exchange for the promise to Christianize the Indians, when in fact the pope's temporal power was limited and did not include the right to make that dona-tion.[9] Vitoria also criticized the manner in which the Conquest was undertaken. But in the end he also argued that in certain circum-stances, war was justified—in order to free the Indians from despotic rule of, say, Mexica emperors, in the case of human sacrifice or can-nibalism, or when the Indians impeded the preaching of Christianity.

In the 1520s, almost immediately after the Conquest of Mexico, the Franciscans became engaged in a parallel debate about the educa-tion of the Indians. How would a population that spoke Nahuatl and other languages learn about Christianity? Were the Indians humans? Could they become complete and fully realized Christians? Fray Pedro de Gante established a school in Texcoco; shortly thereafter, in Mexico-Tenochtitlan, the Franciscans established a school for Indians, San José de los Naturales; and in 1536 the Colegio de la Santa Cruz was founded in Tlatelolco.[10] Franciscans, as well as Dominicans and Augustinians, began to study native languages like Nahuatl, Purépe-cha, Otomí, Zapotec, Mixtec, and Maya and to produce a corpus of primers on the Catholic faith in various Indian languages.

The discussion that follows is a translation of Castro's defense of Indian intellect and education. Little attention has been given to Cas-tro as a defender of the Tlatelolco project or his role in the broader debate about Indian humanity. While he never mentions Tlatelolco by name, it is clear that he has it in mind when discussing the issue of Indian education. It is a monument to the diversity of early mod-ern Spanish thought that a man like Castro, an admirer of Erasmus but a bitter opponent of Luther, a defender of the Inquisition but a liberal theologian, would offer such a vigorous and intense defense of the right of Indians to pursue the priesthood.

Castro outlines the objections that his opponents raised to educat-ing the Indians in Latin and theology: the Indians were inconstant, idolatrous, and prone to polytheism and perverse rites. Not so, responds Castro. Castro's discussion is academic, but one sees some of the traits that must have made him such a successful preacher: he

9. See Francisco de Vitoria, *Political Writings*, ed. Anthony Pagden and Jeremy Lawrance (Cambridge: Cambridge University Press, 1991).

10. See Osorio Romero, *La enseñanza del latín a los indios;* and Kobayashi, *La educación como conquista.*

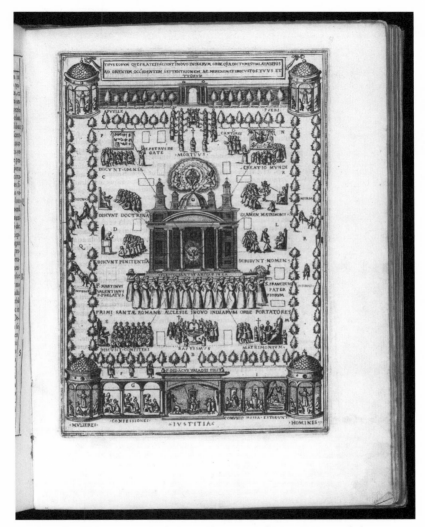

Fig. 1 Idealized Franciscan educational compound. From Diego Valadés, *Rhetórica christiana* (1579). Courtesy Beinecke Rare Book and Manuscript Library, Yale University.

had a real ear for the colloquial and was an effective user of bombast, which serves some preachers' styles. He does not mince words, calling the opponents of Indian education brutish, un-Christian, reactionary, and superstitious, jealous guardians of their Indian charges like landlords with serfs, irrational keepers of an academic mafia.

Castro also makes a vigorous argument against the prohibitions on new Christians rising in the Church hierarchy. While he does not go so far as to attack blood purity statutes, it is clear that Castro viewed them suspiciously. He looks to the early Church and the Book of Acts to argue that if new Christians or converts had been denied a role in the early Church, there would never have been a Church. After all, virtually all the earliest propagators of the Church had been either new Christians or converts from Judaism.

The earliest version we have of the document that is reproduced here is an elegantly penned manuscript. It is clearly a copy, as the individual signatures of various theologians who signed their approvals all appear in the same hand. It is not entirely clear if Castro himself physically copied the manuscript or if a professional scribe did so. The manuscript is found in Archivo General de las Indias, Seville, Indiferente 858. A transcription of the Latin is found in Juan B. Olaechea Labayen, *Anuario de estudios americanos* 15 (1958). A bilingual Latin-Spanish version was produced by Ignacio Osorio Romero in *La enseñanza del latín a los indios* (1990). I have relied on all three versions in an attempt to produce an accurate English rendering.

The list of those who endorsed the brief is telling. Vitoria, the master of the emerging Thomist school of Salamanca, wonders, in his endorsement, what kind of irrational theologian would oppose the education of the Indians. This is not in itself especially astonishing. Even though Vitoria was a Dominican, Castro was never himself attacked as suspiciously Erasmian or humanist, and he seems to have had the support of Vitoria on this issue. Likewise, Vitoria was well known to be a supporter not only of the dominion of the Indians but also of their intelligence—one of his principal arguments in *De indis* was that societies like the Mexica proved that they had a system of government as a precursor to dominion.

But the brief is signed by more controversial characters. Constantino Ponce de la Fuente, like Castro, had studied at the humanist university at Alcalá. He was favored, like Castro, by Emperor Charles V, and was later named the preacher of the Seville Cathedral. Along with Juan Gil (Dr. Egidio), who cosigned his approval with De la Fuente, he was accused of being part of the Lutheran circle in Seville in the 1550s. When the reactionaries finally struck, under the leadership of the archbishop of Seville and inquisitor general, Fernando de Valdés, the Inquisition entered its most vigorous activity in decades. The primate of the Spanish Church, the archbishop of Toledo, Bartolomé de Carranza, a humanist Dominican, was arrested, accused of heresy, and held in prison in Spain and Rome for seventeen years while his trial wound through various legal, diplomatic, and political machinations.[11] And in Valladolid and Seville, massive purges of the suspected Lutheran groups were undertaken. Both Egidio and Constantino were implicated in the Spanish Inquisition's attack on the supposed Lutheran circles in Seville. Constantino was imprisoned by the Inquisition in 1558 and died in 1560 in the inquisitional jail awaiting trial. Egidio was tried in absentia and burned in effigy as a heretic in 1560 in Seville.[12]

Others signed the piece in approval. Fray Andrés Vega was a student of Vitoria and Castro in Salamanca. He took the Franciscan habit in 1538 and died in 1549. Fray Francisco Castillo was likewise a Franciscan and a known opponent of Erasmus. Fray Luis de Carvajal too was a Franciscan and an outspoken opponent of Erasmus, as well as a fervent supporter of the Immaculate Conception. Castro thus had support across a wide range of theological positions and viewpoints concerning Erasmus, humanism, and reform of the Catholic Church.[13]

It remains a bit of a mystery whether the manuscript is Castro's own copy. The accepted view is that the manuscript is a faithfully made copy. But there are no notary's remarks, no notary's signature. Castro does add some comments at the end about the difficulty of finding "learned scribes," implying that he penned the copy himself. This is a carefully redacted copy, since none of those who signed their approval did so in their own hands. It is possible also that Castro penned the discussion and then seamlessly added a dictation of the responses. The placement of the manuscript in the Indiferente section

11. See the classic study of the trial by José Ignacio Tellechea Idígoras, *El arzobispo Carranza y su tiempo*, 2 vols. (Madrid: Ediciones Guardarrama, 1968), as well as the more recent *El arzobispo Carranza "Tiempos recios,"* 4 vols. (Salamanca: Publicaciones Universidad Pontificia; Fundación Universitaria Española, 2003–2007), and discussion of the trial by the prosecutor in the case, Diego de Simancas, "La vida y cosas notables del señor Obispo de Zamora don Diego de Simancas . . . ," in *Autobiografías y memorias*, ed. M. Serrano y Sanz (Madrid: Bailly, Bailliére é hijos, 1905).

12. Marcel Bataillon, *Erasmo y España: Estudios sobre la historia espiritual del siglo XVI*, trans. Antonio Alatorre, 524–40 (Mexico City: Fondo de Cultura Económica, 1966).

13. Bataillon, *Erasmo y España*, passim.

of the Archivo General de las Indias gives little indication either way, as the document that precedes it does not appear to have any relation to the Castro discussion.

The work may have been a brief (*parecer*) generated for distribution or as copy for potential publication. But we cannot entirely dismiss the possibility of some fraud, though it is unlikely. The labor that went into penning it, while nothing like that which went into preparing a lengthy commentary book, was hardly insubstantial, and claiming credit for it in the name of a well-known ally of the Crown would have been risky—to say nothing of forging the names of other well-heeled theologians.

In the translation that follows, I have aimed for readability over literalness. Abbreviations of theological and biblical citations are spelled out, and I have placed citations that do not occur in the original in brackets to indicate that they are my addition.

Alfonso de Castro
"On Whether the Indians of the New World Should Be Instructed in Liberal Arts and Sacred Theology" (1543)

I have been asked whether the men of the New World, who are commonly called Indians, who have left the devil for Christ and received baptism and sworn to this, should be instructed in what are called the liberal arts and taught sacred theology, and whether all the mysteries of our faith should be revealed to them.

It is hardly ridiculous that among the many issues of dispute brought forth for consideration, we consider this question in particular. The first issue of dispute is that the men in those regions are by their nature unstable and faithless and even recently persisted in that same state of faithlessness. Therefore, many assert and fear that the Indians could quickly and easily revert to the former primitive vices, idolatry, and veneration of relics to which they were given before they were baptized. Thus, many say that unless God averts it they will then attack us with our own weapons once they have obtained them. For with those same liberal arts and doctrines learned from us they will attack us and condemn and mock the mysteries of our faith which they learned from the sacred Scripture. If this comes to pass, they will reduce everything great in our faith to meagerness and demolish it.

Moreover, Our Savior says in Matthew, "Do not give what is holy to dogs or throw your pearls before swine, lest they trample them underfoot, and turn and tear you to pieces."[14] Consequently, because the mysteries of our faith are holy and indeed true pearls, it follows that they must not be cast before these same men, who, given the obscenity of their vices, must be deemed impudent dogs and abominable swine.

For even the tools used in the tabernacle of the Old Law were not revealed to everyone. These tools were placed in the Ark of the Covenant, and when they were moved along with the encampment they were rolled up personally by Aaron and those who served in the tabernacle so that the general populace did not see them. Not even those who carried the Ark of the Covenant on their own shoulders and who would sacrifice their lives for it saw them.[15] But holy books are like those implements in which the mysteries of our faith are contained. Therefore, those holy books must be kept secret from the populace and under no circumstance should they be entrusted to them to read. These are, according to my judgment, the things that could in some way favor this opinion.

But even with these objections I would openly provide the contrary conclusion. In order that I might vigorously and clearly offer my conclusion on this subject, first I will argue that the secrets of theology and the mysteries of the faith must be revealed to the Indians. Thereafter I will discuss, by my meager faculties and intelligence, whether men of such character should be instructed in the liberal arts.

The mysteries of our faith are many and varied. Some are those which all Christians must know, without the knowledge and confession of which no one can truly be called a Christian. These are all those mysteries contained in the work of the apostles. These—and if by chance there are others of the same quality—must be revealed to everyone without distinction. No one who has come to the use of reason can be admitted to holy baptism until they have completely learned these basic mysteries and placed complete faith in them. Thus, Our Savior Christ most admirably taught that this must be

14. In the margin: Matthew 8 [i.e., 7:6]. Bible translations are from the New American Bible unless otherwise noted.

15. In the margin: Numbers 4.

done when, on ascending to heaven, he told his apostles, "Go into the whole world and proclaim the gospel to every creature. Whoever believes and is baptized will be saved."[16]

He ordered the Gospel preached—not the sect of Aristotle or Plato or any other such philosopher. While the works of the philosophers should not be disdained, their works are not necessary for salvation. But without knowledge of the Gospel no one can achieve true salvation of the soul, for Christ ordered the apostles to preach the Gospel not in this or that corner of the world, but in the entire world; nor did he order the apostles to preach the Gospel among this or that nation but to all peoples so that all creatures might hear it. Christ excluded no nation, no people from hearing the Gospel—not Indians, not Scythians, not Arabs, not Sarmatians, not even Jews or Greeks, as Paul thus best expresses: "For there is no distinction between Jew and Greek; the same Lord is Lord of all, enriching all who call upon him."[17] Therefore, the Gospel must be preached to all peoples so that they can be saved.

Furthermore, what should be determined by the authors of the Gospel in order that those men obtain salvation is made clear by the sequence of words thus expressed: "Whoever believes and is baptized will be saved."[18] By these words expressed in the preaching of the Gospel, Christ explained that baptism and faith are necessary for salvation. Because he mentioned faith before baptism, he taught that sacred baptism should not be administered to those who have the use of reason if beforehand they refuse to acknowledge faith in the Gospel.

Therefore, first the Indians must be instructed in the true and Catholic faith, and they should be examined in it before they are cleansed by baptism. If, in the last moments of life, an Indian should ask for baptism with a burning desire, explaining that he wishes to profess and confirm Christianity and die as a Christian, such a man should be baptized instantly. Although such a person would not be completely instructed in the faith, it is sufficient that one is prepared to believe what the Church believes.

There are other, more secret mysteries of our faith. Not all should have knowledge of these. This is because without the knowledge and

16. In the margin: Mark [16:15–16].
17. In the margin: Romans 10[:12].
18. Mark 16:16.

confession of these more difficult and secret mysteries man may still obtain eternal life as long as he is prepared to believe them with his heart and confess them by mouth once they are preached to him by someone whom he is obligated to believe.

Many of these mysteries are contained in sacred works and have been deduced by sacred doctors of the Church from the contents of Holy Scripture. For example, three persons beget in one origin three creations; the Father and the Son are one beginning in the production of the Holy Spirit. Any one of the divine persons exists in the other two persons. The human nature of Christ is derived from the Son, who does not completely derive from the Father and the Holy Spirit. Thus, that which was mere bread before consecration is not reduced to nothing in the Eucharist but rather fundamentally transformed into another substance.[19]

It is not urgently necessary that the faithful understand all of these mysteries in order to achieve eternal salvation. Therefore, such mysteries should not be preached publicly and indiscriminately to all believers or to the unlearned, nor should they be freely imparted to the ignorant multitude even if they are born of old Christians. I make no distinction on that score between old and new Christians, because whoever is born of Christian parents, when he should hear something which surpasses his intelligence and thereafter cannot

19. The debate over transubstantiation of the Eucharist was among the most heated in the mid-sixteenth century. Many of the more radical reformers (Protestant) rejected entirely the notion that the host miraculously transformed into the body of Christ, as the wine did into the blood of Christ. Yet a surprising number of Catholics either doubted this transformation or did not fully understand the metaphysics. Catholic theologians had a difficult time explaining this to the laity, and the Inquisition made the denial of transubstantiation one of the heresies that it prosecuted with regularity.

Likewise, in the Americas this became one of the battlegrounds in the Christianization efforts. There was an intense debate about the extent to which Indians should be instructed in the mysteries and metaphysics of the Eucharist. It was motivated, to an extent, by fears on the part of Catholic clergy about Indians "backsliding" into ritual cannibalism and human sacrifice, given that the Catholic view of the Eucharist could be associated with cannibalism. At the same time, given the attacks by radical reformers from Switzerland on the Eucharist, Catholic missionaries found themselves in the tricky position of having to choose between promoting one of the principal sacramental defenses against the reformers and leaving the Indians out of the discussion. Some went so far as to argue that the Indians should not be allowed to receive the Eucharist at all. For discussions, see Pardo, *Origins of Mexican Catholicism*; and Josep Ignasi Saranyana, "La eucaristía en la teología sacramentaria Americana del siglo XVI," in *Eucaristía y nueva evangelización: Actas del IV Simposio la Iglesia en España y América: Siglos XVI–XX* (Córdoba: CajaSur Obra Social y Cultural, 1994).

understand it very well, may still fall into other errors. Frequently such a person falls into error with the same ease as someone who, whether born of Christian or Jewish parents, has only recently accepted Christianity.[20]

One must consider the condition of the audience, and the words of the preacher must be tempered according to the variety of the audience.[21] Ideas must be preached to the unskilled and ignorant people in the clearest and simplest sense, for Paul, writing thus to the Corinthians, gave witness that he did the same with them: "Brothers, I could not talk to you as spiritual people, but as fleshly people, as infants in Christ."[22] Interpreting these words in his commentaries on the Letters of Paul, Anselm [sic] asserts, "For the souls of the audience must not be taken beyond their capacities. Some listeners can be exposed to eminent and high ideas little by little while on the other hand only simple ideas, and not high and mystical ones, should be preached to neophytes since they are weak. But to the true student profound and mystical ideas must be taught."[23] And Saint Paul [sic] warns those same listeners how they must be directed to the meaning by way of the simplest topics, saying thus: "like newborn infants, long for pure spiritual milk."[24]

Before a learned and expert assembly one must dispute in a more complex way, lest the simplicity of the themes move the audience to boredom. Speaking to the apostles, Christ said, "Knowledge of the

20. The attack on those who, in Spain, stuck to a hard-line view of the "impurity" of New Christians (i.e., those with some Jewish or *converso* lineage) would have struck a raw nerve, though Vitoria, as well as Saint Teresa of Avila, were well known to have *converso* or Jewish ancestors.

21. A standard refrain of Thomist hierarchy of knowledge that was systematized most notably by Aquinas in *Summa theologiae*, especially in 2a.2ae., ar. 10, qu. 7. Castro comments extensively on this section of Aquinas and on the broader implications of theological debate, whether it should be public or not, and the quality of the audience. This was also informed, no doubt, by his extensive experience as a preacher in Salamanca.

22. In the margin: 1 Cor. 3[:1].

23. Castro attributes this to Anselm, but it is actually from the twelfth-century Benedictine Herveus Burgidolensis, in his *Commentaria in epistolas Pauli, in epist. I ad Cor.,* found in PL, vol. 181, 837. Castro may have relied on a 1533 Paris edition of these commentaries attributed to Anselm. See Juan B. Olaechea Labayen, "Opinión de los teólogos españoles sobre dar estudios mayores a los Indios," *Anuario de estudios americanos* 15 (1958): 66n6. Translations from works cited by Castro are by the author unless otherwise noted.

24. In the margin: I Peter 2[:2].

mysteries of the kingdom of God has been granted to you; but to the rest, they are made known through parables."[25] Therefore, it should be decided in the clearest way what should be the public preaching of the word of God to that unlearned populace found in the New World. Only those mysteries of the faith necessary to attain eternal life must be preached to that populace. They must be instructed in virtues and vices so that being able to distinguish the one from the other virtue is fortified and the perpetuation of vices is hindered.

But other, more secret mysteries must not be revealed to the Indians in ordinary preaching. Nonetheless, I think that this law does not have to be observed in the schools. Ordinary preaching is one thing, but scholarly training is another, and what is appropriate for one does not necessarily apply to the other. Many different kinds of people attend common preaching, and although many learned men might be present, the great majority of the audience is composed of foolish and ignorant men. Therefore, in common preaching one must address the mental abilities of the many rather than only look to the few.

But when the doctrine is taught in the schools, such variety and quantity of individuals do not attend. Therefore, the theological doctor can better distinguish the qualities of each of the listeners and thus can, according to the condition of the listeners, temper the doctrine accordingly. In common preaching the preacher does not speak to one or the other but rather simultaneously to all. Even when he says something that only applies to one of the listeners, he says it as it if pertained to all. The pulpit does not allow the preacher to question listeners or the audience to respond in such a way that the preacher can discern who is benefitting from hearing the word of God.

The scholastic doctor observes a law contrary to all these. Although sometimes he speaks simultaneously to all, on other occasions he speaks to and questions each individual student. He can determine the level of skill of each one and come to know who is ignorant and thus put to him only ideas which he can easily understand. If, on the other hand, he distinguishes more apt pupils, he can put more difficult questions to them.

It should be added that those who attend schools, especially those who study theology, are required to have studied some other science previously and are not, in general, as ignorant and misinformed as

25. In the margin: Luke 8[:10].

those who attend popular and common preaching. Consequently, those of less mental capacity, their debility being revealed, are moved back and do not advance in the study of letters, or they move to some easier subject. For these reasons it is clear that in the schools many ideas can be discussed and taught which are prohibited in common preaching. Thus, while the highest and most secret mysteries of our faith must not be discussed in the popular preaching before the recently converted Indians, this does not hinder the theological doctor from teaching those mysteries in the schools and revealing them to those who are competent to receive them. For many people say that there are among the Indians those to whom God endowed a sharp intellect and who understand very difficult concepts explained to them.

In his letters Saint Paul deals with the highest and most secret mysteries of our faith, and he considers in them such difficult questions that even to this day they bedevil and confuse the minds of many learned men and true faithful believers. For in those letters Paul deals with subjects like original sin, predestination, grace and free will, faith and works, not putting all our confidence in our merits, the cessation of legal ceremonies with the priest in their place, the excellence of virginity over marriage, marriage celebrated among the faithful and how and when it remains a unity, and many other issues of this kind, all of which a diligent and attentive reader of these letters will easily grasp.

Nevertheless, all these subjects could present considerable difficulty, as indicated by so many questions presented on them by the faithful and so many manifest differences among learned men. Not without reason Saint Peter the apostle said, "speaking of these things as he [Paul] does in all his letters. In them there are some things hard to understand that the ignorant and unstable distort to their own destruction."[26]

Yet Saint Paul wrote these letters not for old Christians but for neophytes, not only for the bishops of the cities but for all the common people, not only for the constant and firm in the faith but also for the vacillating and for those who threaten ruin and for those who have left the faith.[27] According to him, the Galatians, for whom he wrote, had strayed from the true faith toward another gospel.

26. In the margin: 1 Peter 3 [i.e., 2 Peter 3:16].
27. In the margin: Galatians 1.

Therefore, just as Paul, when writing to neophytes, dealt with such high mysteries and occupied himself with such difficult questions, it is suitable that those who dedicate their lives to preaching the Gospel to the Scythians or the Sarmatians or any other peoples make an effort to imitate Paul and work according to the example that he provided for us in his letters. After one has explained the rudimentary principles of our faith to all those who wish to receive the faith of Christ, one should choose some of those who are proven in the faith and customs and shown to be firm in faith and sharp in intellect. At this point reveal to them the highest mysteries and secrets of the faith, explain its most complicated intricacies, and interpret the Holy Scripture and the true theology so that thus instructed they can instruct others.

Expounding on the Song of Solomon, "If there is a wall we will build ramparts on it,"[28] Cassiodorus asserts, "when my apostles began to preach to the church united from various peoples, if the listeners were of such a nature that they could be called a perfect wall, and understood so much that they were endowed with a natural intellect or excel in philosophical erudition, they can in a certain way defend and protect others, as with a wall we build fortifications on that same wall, that is, we deliver to them the words of the divine scripture."[29] It must be stressed that those words tell those listeners of the word of God who had been endowed with natural intellect that they must then be entrusted with the knowledge of the Holy Scripture so that they can then protect others.

But among the Indians there are many who, if they were taught, could optimally understand the Holy Scripture. It is suitable to teach them so that they can teach and defend others. Paul also teaches that this must be done, and writing to Timothy he says, "And what you heard from me through many witnesses entrust to faithful people who will have the ability to teach others as well."[30] However, those

28. In the margin: Can. [i.e., Song of Songs or Song of Solomon] 8[:9]. The translation here follows the Vulgate as Castro gives it.

29. This comes from the commentaries on the Song of Solomon attributed to Cassiodorus (Flavius Magnus Aurelius Cassiodorus), statesman and then monk, active in the sixth century in the Ostrogoth kingdom and later in Byzantium: *Expositio in Cantica Canticorum*, PL, vol. 70, 1103. For discussion see Ann W. Astell, "Cassiodorus's *Commentary on the Psalms* as an *Ars rhetorica*," *Rhetorica* 17 (1999); and James J. O'Donnell, *Cassiodorus* (Berkeley: University of California Press, 1979).

30. In the margin: 2 Tim. 2[:2].

whom Paul orders to be instructed for the office of teacher were at
that time new Christians. Thus, the religion would multiply and
grow with our true doctrine. The apostle Paul did not doubt that they
should be thus instructed in order that later they could be teachers
for others. On the other hand, how can such a great multitude be
taught by so few, unless those who now teach in turn instruct others
to receive the office of teacher? Thus, the teachers being multiplied,
the number of faithful also thus multiplies.

"The harvest is abundant," says the Lord, "but the laborers are
few."[31] The great harvest, Saint Jerome interprets, is the crowd of all
believers, whereas the few workers are those apostles who are the
Lord's imitators sent to the harvest.[32] Accordingly, given this multitude
of people, it is fitting that all work follow the advice of the Savior, who
says, "ask the master of the harvest to send out laborers for his harvest."[33] We should pray to God that there are many who want to teach
those Indians to raise from those stones some sons of Abraham who
would like to teach others the Catholic faith and be confirmed in it.

Nevertheless, those who think that the Holy Scripture and the
true theology should not be revealed to the Indians, nor that the role
of teacher be entrusted to them, perhaps only do so because they
want to assert that role with great pride and arrogance. They deny
this to the Indians precisely because a good deal of their authority would diminish if everyone did not need to depend on them or
if everyone did not need their teaching when there are others who
could teach them.

If this is the case, they are very far indeed from Christ, the master
of all, who fled from this arrogance, although he alone would have
been enough for the entire harvest, even if it were great. Nonetheless
he sent other operatives to the harvest—the apostles. The venerable
Chrysostom in Homily 33 on Saint Matthew asserts, "Look how
he flees from the inane glory of men and how much he denigrates
ostentation, for he sent the disciples so that not everyone would flock
to him."[34]

That deacon Philip, who, inspired by the Holy Spirit, climbed into
the chariot which bore the eunuch of Candace, queen of Ethiopia, did

---

31. In the margin: Matthew 9[:37].
32. Cf. Jerome, *Commentaria in Evangelium Mathei* 1:9, PL, vol. 26, 60.
33. Matthew 9:38.
34. Cf. Chrysostom, *Homilia* 32, PG, vol. 57.

not prohibit or dissuade that eunuch in any way from reading the Prophet Isaiah; rather, he clarified the passage of Isaiah which he read and took the opportunity to teach him the faith in Christ, of which Isaiah prophesied in that passage.[35] If he did not prohibit this eunuch, still unbaptized, from reading Scripture but rather explained it to him, there is no reason that Holy Scripture should not be explained and that other mysteries of the faith not be revealed to the Indians who are already converted.

It is also possible that the same Indians, not tolerating the domination of the Spaniards, with no injury to the Catholic faith, may shake off the yoke of the king of Spain. Indeed this same thing happens daily among the Italians, who, with no damage to the Catholic faith, fight to free themselves from the old yoke of domination and then immediately enter into a new one.[36]

It is also possible that, because God thus orders or allows it, the Indians, with no detriment to the Catholic faith, beheading all the Spaniards that are now in the Indies or killing them by any other manner, close the entrance to any other foreign peoples. If that were to pass, the Catholic faith would die completely among them, as none of those who remained would be able to teach them since all would only have received the rudiments of the faith, and many would then fall easily into several errors. In this manner, in the future the Catholic faith could be abolished.

Today there are many such examples in Asia of people who remain Christian only in name, who, because they do not have anyone among them to teach them, mix many errors into their faith. For example, the Maronites sent an ambassador to Leo X to ask for learned men to teach them the true and Catholic faith, since among them no one had remained who could teach faithfully, and they believed that for this reason they had erred in many things.[37]

---

35. In the margin: Acts 8. This refers to the story of Philip, who converted the eunuch of Candace.

36. Castro refers here to the frequent battles between Spain and France for dominance in various Italian principalities like Sardinia, Sicily, and Naples. As Castro wrote his discussion, Charles V and Francis I had been confronting each other.

37. The Maronites are a sect named after Saint Maron (martyred ca. 410), a friend and contemporary of Saint John Chrysostom. The church is based in Lebanon. Given its traditional location between the Turks, Islam, and the Eastern Church, the sect was viewed as "squeezed" between various hostile groups. Leo X remarked of it, "It is a rose among thorns, an impregnable rock in the sea, unshaken by the enraged waves

This too could happen among the Indians. Therefore, I think it is necessary to create theological doctors from their own people so that if learned men ceased to travel from Europe to the New World, they would not die for lack of the word of God. We should not simply consider the present but also look to the future. If the apostles and other disciples of the Lord had not created teachers among those who converted to the faith in Christ because of their preaching, who, once the apostles died, would have been able to teach others? They would have immediately returned to their first blindness, for which we can justifiably teach from Isaiah, "Unless the LORD of hosts had left us a scanty remnant, we had become as Sodom, we should be like Gomorrah."[38] Therefore, in order that the Indians do not become like Sodom and Gomorrah, those who currently instruct the Indians should elevate some of them to the office of doctor, so that like a seed they will bear fruit.

It is worth adding that those thus indoctrinated not only can take advantage to teach the rest of the populace contents of the Catholic faith but can also instruct them in royal power, so that it is conserved as best as possible in its dominion and power.[39] For the Holy Scripture and the Catholic faith teach that obedience should be given not only to good and modest superiors but also to the wayward. And thus Paul asserts, "whoever resists authority opposes what God has appointed, and those who oppose it will bring judgment upon themselves."[40]

For these and many other reasons it is fitting that true theology be taught, and that the Indians be instructed in true theology and Holy Scripture to preserve not only the Catholic faith but also royal power. For it is a given that those who would have been instructed will better maintain the others united in obedience to the king. Thus, Solomon asserts in Proverbs, "Arrogant men set the city ablaze, but wise men calm the fury."[41]

In the earliest times of the Church it was customary to have a public school in which the new Christians were instructed according

---

and fury of the thundering tempest." Cited in Tobia Anaissi, *Bullarium Maronitarum* (Rome: n.p., 1922), n.p. Also see Kamal Suleiman Salibi, *A House of Many Mansions: The History of Lebanon Reconsidered* (London: I. B. Tauris, 1988), 72.

38. In the margin: Isaiah 1[:9].
39. In the margin: 1 Peter 2.
40. In the margin: Romans 13[:2].
41. Proverbs 29:8.

to the capacity of each individual. Some were instructed in the lowest mysteries of the faith, others in more elevated ones. On recalling the School of Alexandria, and speaking of Pantaenus in his book on the Writings of the Holy Fathers [*De viris illustribus*], Jerome asserts, "according to an old custom of Alexandria, where the ecclesiastics were always doctors since Saint Mark the Evangelist, Pantaenus, philosopher of the Stoic sect, had such prudence and learning both in divine Scripture and in secular literature, that legates of those people asked Demetrius, bishop of Alexandria, that he send him to India." A little further Jerome adds, "Many of his commentaries on Holy Scripture remain, but the living voice was much more useful in the churches. He taught in the time of Prince Severus and Antoninus Caracalla."[42]

Here you see that in the time of the apostles Alexandria had doctors who taught publicly. But as Eusebius of Caesarea says much more amply and openly than Jerome in book 4, chapter 10 of his *Ecclesiastical History*, it is important that we listen to him since he speaks of the time of the Emperor Antony.[43] "Pantaenus, that most noble man in all erudition, directed the church school at the same time he exercised the office of doctor. From that time it remains until now the most ancient tradition to have among those, in the church school, as doctors of Divine Scripture, only men most proven in science and erudition." And later in chapter 11 he adds, "In the schools of divine Scripture in Alexandria in particular Clement of Alexandria flourished, who was later called in the city of Rome as much a disciple as a successor of the apostles. This same Clement, in book 7 of his dispositions, calls Pantaenus his master and teacher."[44]

42. This comes from Jerome's *De viris illustribus* 36, PL, vol. 23, 651. An excellent English translation can be found at http://www.newadvent.org/fathers/2708.htm. Caracalla, Roman emperor from 211–217, was born Lucius Septimius Bassianus in 188 and later called Marcus Aurelius Antoninus and Marcus Aurelius Severus Antoninus, was of mixed Syrian and Phoenician descent. The nickname Caracalla ostensibly referred to a kind of Gallic cloak that he habitually wore.

43. Eusebius (ca. 265 to ca. 337–340) is among the best-known historians of the early Church and is often regarded as one of the founders of Church history. He was active in the controversies over Arianism and was an active participant in the Nicene Council of 325, which established the Creed of the Church. He is today known in particular for his *Historiae eclesiasticae* (*Ecclesiastical History*).
The citation here is off: it is book 5, chap. 10 of Eusebius's *Historiae eclesiasticae*, PG, vol. 20, 454. An English version is at http://www.newadvent.org/fathers/250105.htm.

44. Eusebius, *Historiae eclesiasticae* 5.11.

From the preceding you see that in that time the doctors directed public schools in which they taught others and that not only the old Christians were admitted to them but also the new Christians, so that they not only listened but also exercised the office of doctors. Indeed, Pantaenus, so praised by Eusebius, had been a Gentile and a philosopher of the Stoic sect. Likewise, Clement, as the successor to the same Pantaenus in the mastership of the school, testifies, as Eusebius mentions, that among his many masters, he was instructed by one who had come from Hebrew lineage.[45]

In the end, I confirm my opinion with the testimony of Saint Augustine. This most holy and most wise man in that work *De catechizandis rudibus*,[46] writing on the manner in which those who, proceeding from any sect and desiring to be converted to the Christian faith, should be instructed, frequently says that the Holy Scripture should be given to them and interpreted for them each according to their capacities. Demonstrating various questions with which one should interrogate those who are converted to the faith in Christ, he says in chapter 6, "But if it happens that his answer is to the effect that he has met with some divine warning, or with some divine terror, prompting him to become a Christian, this opens up the way most satisfactorily for a commencement to our discourse, by suggesting the greatness of God's interest in us. His thoughts, however, ought certainly to be turned away from this line of things, whether miracles or dreams, and directed to the more solid path and the surer oracles of the Scriptures; so that he may also come to understand how mercifully that warning was administered to him in advance, previous to his giving himself to the Holy Scriptures."[47]

And in chapter 9 on the grammarians and the orators who wish to receive the Christian faith, after which it is determined that they

45. Here Castro attacks the orthodoxy of his day, which insisted on "blood purity" for the priesthood and excluded those of *converso* or Jewish background, and seems to imply his opposition, if only indirectly, to the various statutes that forbade New Christians from holding most ecclesiastical positions.

46. This was a treatise Augustine wrote as a primer in conversion and missionary activities as well as a sophisticated discussion of the process of conscience that a convert was to undergo in order to accept Christianity. Augustine, *De catechizandis rudibus*, PL, vol. 40. The translations in the text from *De catechizandis rudibus* are based on the Reverend S. D. F. Salmond's 1887 translation, which can be found at http://www.ccel.org/ccel/schaff/npnf103.iv.iii.html. The Latin is available at http://www.augustinus.it/latino/catechesi_cristiana/index.htm.

47. Augustine, *De catechizandis rudibus*.

cannot be counted among the ignorant or the learned, he argues, "But above all, such persons should be taught to listen to the divine Scriptures, so that they may neither deem solid eloquence to be mean, merely because it is not inflated, nor suppose that the words or deeds of men, of which we read the accounts in those books, involved and covered as they are in carnal wrappings, are not to be drawn forth and unfolded with a view to an (adequate) understanding of them, but are to be taken merely according to the sound of the letter. And as to this same matter of the utility of the hidden meaning, the existence of which is the reason why they are also called mysteries, the power wielded by these intricacies of enigmatic utterances in the way of sharpening our love for the truth, and shaking off the torpor of weariness, is a thing which the persons in question must have made good to them by actual experience, when some subject which failed to move them when it was placed baldly before them, has its significance elicited by the detailed working out of an allegorical sense. For it is in the highest degree useful to such men to come to know how ideas are to be preferred to words, just as the soul is pre-ferred to the body."[48] And in chapter 16, describing a certain ignorant man not of the countryside but the city, who approached him and wanted to become a Christian, he describes until the end of chapter 24 the discourse that he had been at the point of explaining to that man personally. He explains in this discourse not only the principal rudiments of the faith but also the highest mysteries and secrets of the faith. After dealing with such mystical topics to the end of chap-ter 21,[49] he sends the knowledge of the Holy Scripture, saying thus: "In that land of promise many things were done, which held good as figures of the Christ who was to come, and of the Church, with which you will have it in your power to acquaint yourself by degrees in the Holy Books."

Here you can see how Augustine differs from those who want to prohibit the Indians from having knowledge of Holy Scripture.

48. In this section Augustine develops his position on rhetoric as it relates to Christian faith. Like Plato, Augustine believed that eloquence and rhetoric without moral basis were vain at best and wicked at worst—thus Plato cast the poets out of his ideal republic. Augustine argues along lines also found in the *Gorgias*, in which Socrates attacks the sophists. Castro makes use of both Plato and this section of Augus-tine in making his arguments about censorship and, in particular, the censure of "vain literature" and comedy in *De justa haereticorum punitione*.

49. I.e., chap. 20.

I embrace with much greater enthusiasm the opinion of Augustine than that of those who think that the Indians should be separated from the knowledge of the Holy Scripture and true theology. The opinion of Augustine follows in the footsteps of the apostles. It is close to their doctrine and conforms to the will of Christ, who did not close the door to anyone who wanted to come to him and did not turn his back on anyone who wanted to come to him. To no one who wanted to speak with him did he turn his face away; he did not prohibit anyone from following him. Indeed, when mothers offered their children to Christ so that they would receive blessing from him and the apostles impeded their access, Christ told them, "Let the children come to me, and do not prevent them."[50] Maybe those who maintain the opposite position would say, "We do not prohibit them from going to Christ. Quite the contrary, for we instruct them in the faith, we administer baptism and the other necessary sacraments to them, but we do not prevent them from obtaining a higher state."

To those I say: Why do we dare to impede the promotion of those to whom God not only did not prohibit but indeed invited? Is it not God who, as Job attests, places the humble in the highest place? Does not God raise up the miserable from the dust and the poor from the filth so that they might sit with princes and possess the throne of glory? The people of the New World until now were the miserables and the poor because they lacked those riches of which Solomon says, "A man's riches serve as ransom for his life."[51] Perhaps God now wants to raise up this people from the dung of idolatry and other vices so that they immediately sit and are counted among the first Christians. Perhaps we do not know that God now wants to realize this in them because long ago he prophesied it through Anne, the mother of Samuel: "the hungry batten on spoil. The barren wife bears several sons"?[52] The hungry, explains Angelomus,[53] were the Gentiles deprived of the nourishment of the word of God who later were

---

50. Matthew 19:14.
51. Proverbs 13:8.
52. 1 Samuel 2:5.
53. Angelomus of Luxeuil was a ninth-century Benedictine monk and biblical commentator who wrote a discussion on the books of Samuel and Kings, *Ennarationes in libros regnum* (Rome: Apud Paulum Manutium, 1565), in PL, vol. 115. See Pseudo-Jerome, *Quaestiones on the Book of Samuel by Pseudo-Jerome*, ed. and trans. Avrom Saltman (Leiden: Brill, 1975), and Michael Gorman, "The Commentary on Genesis of Angelomus of Luxeuil and Biblical Studies Under Lothar," *Studi medievali* 40 (1999).

satiated because they fully learned the law of God and understood the other mysteries of the faith.[54] Likewise this body of Gentiles was sterile because it did not bear any son of God. But after the Church was assembled from many Gentiles, the same people who were previously sterile now bear many sons because, through the fount of baptism and preaching of the faith, children were incessantly generated for God. How do we know, then, that God does not want to fulfill this prophecy in the New World as we know it has been fulfilled in Spain and France? Perhaps God rejects the Indians for their sins so that he does not wish to elect from them doctors, preachers, and pastors? Hardly! For as the holy Psalmist says, "You will wash your feet in your enemy's blood; the tongues of your dogs will lap it up."[55] Thus, for those who are in the New World, who until now had been the enemies of God, nothing stands in the way so that God might convert them into hounds who will never cease to bark for him and take the greatest diligence in guarding the dominion of the Church.

Those who wish to alienate the Indians from the reading of the Holy Scripture and the preaching of the Gospel seem to me like that Ananias who refused to place his hands on Paul because of his ancient sins.[56] But seeing that he refused, the Lord said to him, "Go, for this man is a chosen instrument of mine to carry my name before Gentiles, kings, and Israelites."[57] Having heard this, he placed his hands on Paul and was filled with the Holy Spirit. Immediately he began to preach that Jesus was the Son of God, and thus an enemy was converted into a hound and a persecutor into an advocate.

In the ancient times two men, named Eldad and Medad, were preaching in the camps of the children of Israel. "So, when a young man quickly told Moses, 'Eldad and Medad are prophesying in the camp,' Joshua, son of Nun, who from his youth had been Moses' aide, said, 'Moses, my lord, stop them.' But Moses answered him, 'Are you jealous for my sake? Would that all the people of the Lord were prophets! Would that the Lord might bestow his spirit on them all!'"[58] Thus, all those who want to prohibit the Indians from reading the Holy Scripture and the study of theology and the preaching

54. Cf. Angelomus, *Ennarationes in libros regnum* 2.
55. In the margin: Psalm 67 [i.e., 68:23].
56. In the margin: Acts 9.
57. Acts 9:15.
58. In the margin: Numbers 11[:27–29].

of the word of God are like Joshua, who wanted to prohibit from prophesying those to whom God had given the Spirit. But that man who holds the helm of the ship of this subject should, like another Moses, respond, "Would that all the people of the Lord were prophets! Would that the Lord might bestow his spirit on them all!"

Would that the new people of the New World be instructed to such a point in the faith that any of them could teach it. I confess that those who think the opposite, as Paul says, "have zeal for God, but it is not discerning. For, in their unawareness of the righteousness that comes from God and their attempt to establish their own (righteousness), they did not submit to the righteousness of God."[59] As the apostle also says, "the righteousness of God through faith in Jesus Christ [is] for all who believe. For there is no distinction; all have sinned and are deprived of the glory of God."[60]

Until this point I have spoken of the study of sacred theology. Nonetheless, it is not difficult to define whether those other arts, called the liberal arts, should be taught to the Indians, for they prepare the way for theology. These arts, as ancillaries, serve theology as their queen and mistress. All the secular disciplines, as Augustine says so perfectly in book 2, chapter 40 of his *De doctrina Christiana*, are the gold and silver of the Egyptians with which the Tabernacle was created and in which were offered victims and sacrifices to God.[61] For these disciplines prepare the mind for a better understanding of Holy Scripture and the true theology which teaches that the living sacred host, pleasing God, is sacrificed. And as we have demonstrated that with the help of God theology should be interpreted by them, it follows consequently that we must open the other secular disciplines to them in order to prepare the way for the understanding of Holy Scripture and the true theology. For, as Augustine concludes, without these they cannot have a clear and true understanding of Holy Scripture. And, as the saint [Augustine] also reminds us, a great many for their ignorance of the secular disciplines erred gravely in terms of understanding Holy Scripture.

In order that our opinion is made firmly, it is necessary that we respond to the objections and show that they are inane and without force. First, our opponents present, as an obstacle, the inconstancy

59. Romans 10:2–3.
60. Romans 3:22–23.
61. Augustine, *De doctrina christiana*, PL, vol. 34.

and fickleness of the Indians, which they say shows that they daily experiment in many things, and therefore [our opponents] fear that they will be the same in matters of the faith. Therefore, after they receive the faith, but still tied to their original errors, if they learn these liberal arts from us they will turn on us and attack our faith, mock it and scoff at it with the same arts they learned from our sacred books. Oh, most vain argument in which one sins so many times! Let us examine it in its parts, and let us show that there is not a grain of truth in it.

They say that the Indians are inconstant and fickle by their very nature. They say that there are many among them who are fickle. But is it possible that all of them suffer from the same malady? If that is the case, it is astonishing that nature, which is so variable, would not have created a single stolid man. And if some are constant, it is not appropriate to damn them along with the inconstant so that they are denied study along with the others. But let us concede, nevertheless, that all Indians (something which I will never believe) are unstable and fickle in the other human manners. Does this mean we must distrust them equally in matters of the faith? To the contrary. We know of many people who are most fickle in human matters but who are firm and most committed and who would happily offer their necks to the sword before denying the faith. Is it not possible that the faith bestowed in baptism aids nature in such a way that with its help it allows that same nature to become stronger? It advances something, for it diminishes the rebellion of the flesh by making it less harsh, and it tempers concupiscence of the flesh so that it does not burn so hot. Likewise, as it may be believed, it may diminish the stability of the spirit, which is natural in some men, in such a way that the soul better perseveres in good.

Thus, Saint Peter warns that if we are strong in the faith we will resist the devil because he believed that the faith makes us strong.[62] From this Chrysostom deduces, "The nature of the faith is such that as much as it is prohibited it is inflamed that much more. Therefore the servants of God are not defeated by persecution. The virtue of the faith is certain during danger and while in security it is in danger."[63] On the other hand, knowledge also reaffirms the spirit

62. In the margin: 1 Peter 5.

63. It is unclear if this comes from the fragments of Chrysostom's commentaries on the Letter I of Peter or from some other (to date) unidentified source.

and in a certain way strengthens it in order to defend that which we know. For the things which we know with certainty are true we affirm with constancy. And so much more clearly we know the truth itself even though other things are similar. We thus adhere to the truth that much more tenaciously and that much more firmly we affirm the truth. Consequently, those among the Indians who are the most intelligent and learned would also be more constant and firm in the faith than other Indians because they know the truth more clearly. Therefore, in order that the Indians desert that fickleness and inconstancy which their nature gives them, it is fitting that they be instructed more in the faith and its mysteries than other peoples, because, thus more learned in the doctrine and more clearly illuminated, they will more firmly maintain the true faith.

For Saint Paul, writing to Timothy, says, "All scripture is inspired by God and is useful for teaching, for refutation, for correction, and for training in righteousness, so that one who belongs to God may be competent, equipped for every good work."[64] These words were interpreted by Theophylactus in the commentaries on the Letters of Paul, where he says, "If something needs to be corrected or instructed, that is, one should return firmly and soberly to justice and that which is just must be maintained. All this is abundantly given in these holy letters."[65] And Solomon in the Proverbs asserts, "A wise man is more powerful than a strong man, and a man of knowledge than a man of might"[66] Jerome [sic] discusses these words in his commentaries on Proverbs: "Not everyone who is strong is wise. Nonetheless it must be said that anyone who is wise is strong because even if he is weak in body, the presence of wisdom is greater than the strength of his enemies and vanquishes the devil."[67] And [the book of] Ecclesiasticus, speaking of the man who is just and fearful of God, supports this opinion and thus says, "With the bread of life and understanding, she shall feed him, and give him the water of wholesome wisdom to drink: and she shall be made strong in him, and he shall not be moved: And she shall hold him fast, and he shall not be confounded."[68] And in such words Ecclesiasticus teaches clearly that

---

64. In the margin: 2 Tim. 3[:16–17].

65. Found in his *Expositio in epistulam II ad Timoth.* 4, PG, vol. 125.

66. In the margin: Proverbs 24[:5].

67. Castro cites this as Jerome, but it comes from the ninth-century Frankish Benedictine Rabanus Maurus, in his *Expositio in Proverbia Salomensis*, PL, vol. 111, 757.

68. In the margin: Ecclesiasticus 15[:3–4]. Douay-Rheims translation.

man must remain firm in the faith so that he does not waver from the bread of life, which is the true rule of the faith, and the doctrine of the word of God, which is the basis of the life of the soul, and from the water of wholesome wisdom.

So that the Indians remain firm in the faith and do not waver from it, it is necessary that they be fed with the bread of the word of God. Moreover, if they were fickle and inconstant, we should trust in God to change their inconstancy and fickleness into a most firm perseverance. For it is he who, as Job says, makes a weight for the wind,[69] for often he looks at those who are fickle and inconstant like the wind and he, by his grace, leads them to the maturity of perseverance. There are many, as they say, of those who (though God might prevent it) have left the faith which they accepted with baptism. Let us see the extent of their alliance that the sacred theology should not be taught to them, because, they say, weapons should not be given to declared or suspected enemies which they might use to oppose us. But here also they [those who opposed educating the Indians] sin in many ways. The Indians cannot be judged our enemies after they receive the Catholic faith, since they think as we do and serve the same Lord. Nor can they be held as suspected enemies, because he who has not given any hostile sign gives no reason to be suspected of being an enemy. Moreover, according to the Christian rule, anyone who is not proven otherwise must be assumed to be good.

Therefore, those who teach theology to baptized Indians are not giving arms to a declared or suspected enemy. Rather, they are instructing friends for war and providing them with arms with which they can fight even more vigorously for us and for the Catholic faith. In this manner those who say that the Indians, if they leave the faith, will attack the Catholic faith with the same arms we gave them, tremble in fear when there is no reason to tremble. And in order to clarify this point, it is fitting that we ask them for whom do they fear exactly: for God? For the Catholic faith? For the Indians? Or for themselves? If they fear for God, they are fools, for no man or angel sinning or abandoning God hurts God, but only hurts himself. Thus, Augustine in chapter 8[70] of *De catechizandis rudibus* says, "For He who gave freedom of will to men, in order that they might worship God not of slavish necessity but with ingenuous inclination, gave

69. In the margin: Job 28[:25].
70. I.e., chap. 18.

it also to the angels; and hence neither did the angel, who, in company with other spirits who were his satellites, forsook in pride the obedience of God and became the devil, do any hurt to God, but to himself."

Neither do they fear with reason for the Catholic faith, because no conclusion of the Sophists, no fallacy, no argument of the philosophers[71] ever damaged the Catholic faith, and afterward never will be able to damage it. Accordingly, the truth can be attacked, but it cannot be defeated, because it always emerges triumphant. Even though it confronts a thousand strategems and a thousand spears are launched against it, the truth will remain unmoved and fixed until the end of the world because the Lord bore witness that he would ask for the Church not to lose its faith.[72] Therefore, it will never be abandoned as long as he pleads for it, since he is always heard.

And if the opponents of Indian education fear for the Indians themselves, it will be worse for them to have been denied the faith than not to have received it. According to this reason, not only should theology not be taught to the Indians but they should not even be taught the first rudiments of the faith. Nor should they even be given baptism, because it is much worse for them to fall back in the path of truth than never to have entered it in the first place. So if for fear of fickleness and inconstancy they should not be taught, then for the same fear they should never have been baptized. And for fear that the sinner might fall, then he should not have been given absolution.

Let such a pestilent error be far from the hearts of the faithful! For the Wise One counsels that instability should not be taken into consideration when the seed is cast, saying, "One who pays heed to the wind will not sow."[73] Those who conclude that the Indians should not be taught Holy Scripture and theology work only to thwart the planting of the seed because they are left only considering the wind—that is, on considering the inconstancy and fickleness of the Indians, they fail to sow the true doctrine.

But perhaps those who fear for themselves do so because they fear that if the Indians abandon the Catholic faith they will attack them, and thus besieged by the Indians they will then be compelled to abandon the faith. But if this fear stirs them up, this only shows that

71. I.e., pre-Christian thinkers.
72. In the margin: Luke 22.
73. Ecclesiastes 11:4.

they are much more inconstant and fickle than the Indians. And thus we say well that they are stirred up with fear when there is no reason to fear.

They object to us in the second place that one should not give what is holy to dogs or cast pearls before swine.[74] I confess that certainly the divine mysteries, which are indeed true pearls, should not be revealed to the Indians or any other people before baptism. Indeed, if they are given over to idolatry and other obscene vices, they should be judged as dogs and swine. Nevertheless, after having received holy baptism, they should not be considered dogs and swine but rather as children and heirs. For on the other hand neither would it be appropriate, according to this logic, that the first elements of the faith be revealed to them since they are also true pearls.

In the third place they oppose us with the precept of the Old Law which ordered, under penalty of death, that the vessels of the Tabernacle were to be kept hidden so that no one could see or touch them. Nevertheless, we doubly reject this notion so that no one can oppose us. In the first place, according to Augustine, an argument made from mystical sense has no force. Secondly, all those things which were made in the Old Law were like images and shadows of those which would form the evangelic law. It is important to distinguish between the shadow and the body, the image and the truth. Those images and shadows of the future acts were not useful in and of themselves for grace but only had value for their support and devotion of the ministers. For this reason God wanted them to be hidden because if they were shown in public in plain view the objects would have been scorned and worthless. God, as their creator, would have been mocked, especially by those who did not examine the inner mysteries but only saw the exterior shell. Rare things should be held in appreciation, while on the other hand those which are frequently seen then slowly cease to be appreciated. But the mysteries of the New Law are useful in their own right, and the mysteries of the Christian faith are precious on their own. Therefore, they do not need the ornamentation of ceremonies in order to be venerated because they are worthy of veneration on their own. It is not fitting that they be hidden without showing them, especially to those who are capable of appreciating those mysteries, because the things which are truly precious and

74. Matthew 7:6.

beautiful when they are viewed often are praised more because when someone examines them more one finds that much more reason to praise them. For this reason the Holy Eucharist is today publicly shown to the populace, while in antiquity manna, which was an image of the Eucharist, was kept locked in the Ark. Likewise, for this reason all the most secret mysteries of the New Law are revealed which beforehand were prohibited to many because God in his passion removed the veil from us in order that we could see the mysteries more clearly.

These are the things which seem to me, Fray Alonso de Castro, necessary concerning the question under debate. Although many errors of transcription have slipped through for lack of scribes, I do not hesitate to put my pen to this, because these days there is such penury of learned scribes that I do not trust that I could have found someone to whom I could entrust this with confidence. I now understand from my own experience that it is true what Titus Manlius Torquatus says in Livy—that it is difficult to submit to a vow which you carry out with foreign eyes.[75] Fray Alonso de Castro.

All these things said by the reverend father Fray Alonso de Castro appear to me to be excellently, piously, and religiously stated. Moreover, I ask myself who would be the author or inventor of such a dangerous and pernicious opinion to estrange those barbarians from both human and divine education. Certainly not even the devil himself could create a more effective strategy in order to inspire in those people a perpetual hatred for the Christian religion.

   Many have withdrawn from the same Christ the Lord, or from the apostles, but none have ever thought to refuse to transmit the Christian doctrine or deny education to those after receiving the faith. Fray Francisco Vitoria.

Not without reason does the Church complain, through the mouth of the prophet, "Much have they oppressed me from my youth."[76] For many with more zeal than knowledge attack the Church and pretend to defend it. While they labor to save it from only one danger, and

---

75. Cf. Titus Livius, *Ab urbe condita libri* 26.22.
76. Psalm 129:1.

almost always this is a minor one, they allow many extremely grave damages.

They are not far from those ignorant individuals who, taken with their own opinion, do not cease to attack with satanic machinations the recently born Church in the newly discovered western islands and continent. Could there be a crueler and more atrocious fight than to despoil them of true and solid benefits who of their own volition confided in our faith; to enervate all force of wisdom and cast them into chains of ignorance and hurl them into the densest darkness of error? But they could not do so to me, it is said, for though every day impugners of the Church multiply, there is no shortage of those defenders of whom only one defeats many enemies. Nevertheless, there are more with us than against us, and this is due in no small measure to the many and great divine testimonies and of the saints that the reverend father Fray Alfonso de Castro cites here—pious, just, and learned in favor of the doctrine of the Church, which must be supported in this part. We subscribe with great pleasure to his most true and proven opinion, warning those in Christ who sustain the contrary opinion that they cease such a pernicious pledge so that on the judgment day they do not find themselves prisoners of such a harmful and pernicious matter for the dogma. Fray Francisco Castillo. Fray Andrés Vega.

I judge that the inhabitants of the islands and continents of the West must be instructed in good letters and the Holy Scripture. Who are we to make such a distinction if Christ did not do so? Moreover, would we not be in danger of creating a climate of distrust for these new men if they were to see how jealously we hide our mysteries from them? If we do not admit them to the knowledge of the Holy Scripture, it is ridiculous to admit them to baptism, the Eucharist, to absolution and the forgiveness of sins. In reality we would have given what is holy to dogs in this case, since the unworthy are admitted to the participation in the sacraments. For those who are admitted with rights to them are worthy even more of the knowledge of mysteries.

The objections of the adversaries are made in part from ignorance of the Gospel, and in part from human knowledge, which has always opposed the Gospel. In such a fashion it is said that preaching is not led by divine protection but rather that one can govern only with human advice. Thus it happens that men of such a mind, while they wish to appear wise and perspicacious, are in fact sliding toward the blasphemy of infidelity: they do not dare to confide in God. This is my judgment on this subject. Constantino de la Fuente, J. Egidio.

I embrace the opinion of those who say that the *perioikoi*[77] or those of New Spain, who recently swore to the word of Christ, should be admitted to the most secret mysteries of our faith, not only so that they learn them but so that they also can teach them. However, it must always be kept in mind that only those should be allowed who have an advantage in intellect and customs and who love our faith with fervor. On the other hand, I have written on this subject more amply and I refer the reader to this. Nevertheless, I want to place this under the censure of the Church. Seville, La Rábida, January 1543. Fray Luis de Carvajal.

---

77. The word used is *periaecos,* a Latinized version of *perioikoi,* or noncitizen workers of Sparta. The term also refers to those who live on the other side of the world. In this context it means "Indians."

2

In the 1560s, when Alonso Cabello became a Franciscan friar in Mexico City, the order in Mexico was still deeply divided about the role
of Indians in the new Church and about whether they, as well as Africans and mixed-ethnicity peoples, should be admitted to the order.
Some, like Jacobo Daciano, agreed with Castro's view that Indians
should be included as full-fledged members of the Church, but overall
the Franciscans came to oppose this view. Even Sahagún was skeptical
that Indians could become full-fledged members, let alone clergy.

By the 1570s, the Tlatelolco project was in decline, even as
Sahagún's massive undertaking, the Florentine Codex, was coming
to fruition. As early as 1569, many Franciscan friars sent a report
to the Council of the Indies voicing opposition to the project. The
Franciscan order in Mexico was experiencing an internal struggle
about ethnicity and national origin. The presumed racial hierarchy—
of peninsular Spaniards who had professed in Spain (*gachupines*) or
Mexico (*hijos de provincia*), followed by Mexican-born Spaniards
(*criollos*), all of whom ruled over Indians, Africans, and mixed-race
peoples—was challenged, and political rifts developed, as more *hijos
de provincia* and *criollos* joined the order. *Hijos de provincia* made
up well over half the order in Mexico, and *criollos* under 30 percent.
Non-Spaniards, with some exceptions, were excluded.[1]

Cabello, as an *hijo de provincia*, found himself in the middle of
that struggle. In the other major internal division within the Franciscan order in the 1570s, over humanism, the translation of Scripture
into indigenous languages, the influence of Erasmus, and the humanistic goals of the Tlatelolco project, Cabello was in the faction that
held onto a humanistic view of the order.

In 1573, Cabello was residing in Mexico City and studying
theology when various Franciscans began to denounce him to the

---

1. See the discussion in Morales, *Ethnic and Social Background*.

Fig. 2 Grounds of the Franciscan convent of Huaquechula, Puebla, Mexico. Photo: Ryan Crewe.

Inquisition for holding heretical ideas, reading Erasmus, and penning suspicious dialogues. He was imprisoned on May 2, 1573, and interviewed at length by the inquisitor Alfonso Bonilla from May 4 to June 17. During his interrogations before the inquisitor, he admitted to a wide range of heterodox ideas. He said that he thought that many of the rules and ceremonies of the Franciscan order were superstitious and useless, such as eating and sleeping with the friar's hood on one's head. Witnesses said that he refused to observe these rules. Cabello also was found to believe that one should be allowed to leave the Franciscan order freely.

Other damning evidence was offered against him. When his cell in San Francisco in Mexico City was searched after his arrest, among the books found were the *Chiliads* (or *Adagia*) by Erasmus; the *Epítome* on the Italian humanist Lorenzo Valla, also by Erasmus; commentaries on Pauline letters in an edition of Jerome; and commentaries on Cicero—all books either forbidden by the Inquisition (as in the case of the *Chiliads*) or highly suspect, as many Protestant authors had commented on humanist works and on Jerome.

In Cabello's cell was also found a dialogue that Cabello had written entitled "Fict[a]e religionis sphira" (In the realm of the false

Fig. 3 Detail of portico of Franciscan church at Huaquechula, Puebla, Mexico.
Photo: Ryan Crewe.

religion).[2] This would form a central point in the 1573 inquisitional
trial against him. Written in humanistic dialogue form, the "Fict[a]e
religionis sphira" has been described as being "more Erasmian than
Erasmus" by Marcel Bataillon.[3] The dialogue follows closely the various attacks on monasticism that Erasmus had made a half-century

2. AGN, Inq., vol. 116, exp. 1.
3. Bataillon, *Erasmo y España*, 829–31.

earlier and for which his works were condemned. Cabello thus used this manuscript to propose a variety of suspect ideas: that Franciscans should be free to marry; that each convent needed only one priest; that monasticism was useless; that the state of monasticism was otiose and sinful. Cabello also says in the dialogue that "of the time we spend as monks, part of it is dedicated to the charms of life and the other part to the arrogance of empire."[4] These propositions were subjected to close scrutiny by the Inquisition's censors, who considered most of them heretical or at least "erroneous, scandalous, offensive to pious ears, and smacking of the Lutheran heresy."

Of the censors, a Franciscan, Antonio de Quixada, tended to offer the most negative assessments of Cabello's ideas. Here is an intersection between several of the Franciscans in this volume. Quixada had been a student of Alfonso de Castro in Salamanca before going to Mexico, had spent time in the Yucatán, and was guardian of the Franciscan house in Guatemala in 1557 when he acted as a censor in the witchcraft trial against Doña María de Ocampo.[5] Quixada settled in Mexico City and was appointed a permanent censor of the Inquisition in 1572.[6] That Quixada was educated by an admirer of Erasmus, Castro, and would then provide the most trenchant criticism of another admirer of Erasmus, Cabello, underscores the ideological complexity of the Franciscan order and of its relationship with Erasmian thinking. For example, in the winter of 1571–72 the Dominican censor of the Mexican Inquisition, Bartolomé de Ledesma, undertook a general inspection of private libraries in central Mexico in an effort to rid them of prohibited books. All the Franciscan friaries were found to possess prohibited books by Erasmus.[7] It is clear that there was a wide net of support for Erasmus within the Franciscan order in Mexico in the 1570s, and Cabello was the beneficiary of this indulgence of illegal books. But there was also clearly an anti-Erasmian faction among the Mexican Franciscans, and Cabello in many ways became the scapegoat offered to this faction by the pro-Erasmians.

Eventually Cabello saw the scales tipping against him and opted for a full mea culpa before the inquisitor, admitting to heresy and

4. AGN, Inq., vol. 116, exp. 1, fol. 53: "nostra etate monachum esse, partim pertinet ad vitae illecebram, partim ad insolens imperium."

5. AGN, Inq., vol. 40, exp. 35.

6. AGN, Inq., vol. 35, exp. 2; vol. 63, exp. 18.

7. AGN, Jesuitas, III-26, exp. 22.

Erasmianism. He was convicted as a heretic, which on its own was severe because any recidivism could result in a death penalty sentence, and sentenced to three years of house arrest, which he completed in Cholula. During this time he was stripped of his voting rights within the order and ordered to occupy himself with the "lowest" occupations within the convent, which in theory meant menial labor intended to humiliate him.[8]

The punishment of Cabello seems to have sparked a wide-scale controversy within the Franciscan order in Mexico. As early as October 1574, Quixada reported to the Inquisition that Cabello continued to have access to Erasmus's works; he also presented various manuscripts that Cabello had penned. At the same time, Fray Miguel de Zárate reported that despite the warnings, Cabello continued to share Erasmus's books, such as his *Letters,* in Cholula.[9] Cabello was also found to have other suspicious books in his cell, such as editions by Ovid, the humanist Luis Vives, and Lorenzo Valla.

The Inquisition did not order a trial at this stage, but by the late spring of 1578 some members of the order had run out of patience. Fray Juan Bastida, the guardian of the Cholula house, had allowed Cabello to teach grammar there. What seemed to tip the scales was that near Christmas 1577 Bastida had allowed Cabello to preach the Nativity sermon at Cholula. In response, those who did not share the Erasmian or humanist leanings of some members of the order initiated an investigation against Cabello, with the *comisario general* of the Franciscans in Mexico, Fray Rodrigo de Seguera, conducting an in-house investigation. Seguera interviewed various friars from Cholula, most of whom had been present at Cabello's sermon. Seguera, for one, was enraged that Bastida had allowed Cabello to preach given his previous conviction by the Inquisition—an opinion shared by Fray Antonio de Rueda, who suggested that Cabello ought to have been performing chores like cooking and doorkeeping. Rueda seemed especially incensed that Cabello did not cross himself before beginning the sermon.[10]

Seguera went to the Inquisition with the results of his in-house investigation in late summer 1578, and Cabello was ordered apprehended. Once again, when Cabello was arrested, his room was

8. AGN, Inq., vol. 116, exp. 1.
9. AGN, Inq., vol. 88, exp. 1.
10. Ibid.

searched and a number of prohibited books were found: a Bible with no title page,[11] and various works by Erasmus. There was also a variety of the standard theological and juridical works of the day, including those by Vitoria, De Soto, Covarrubias, and Alonso de la Veracruz.

Cabello was taken to the Franciscan friary in Tlatelolco and placed under house arrest. But in the early morning hours of October 13, 1578, he escaped from his cell, literally by climbing out of his window with a rope. As in the past, Cabello clearly had support from within the Franciscan order. His escape was well planned. A few days before, he was allowed to visit his mother, who gave him sixteen pesos and promised him the use of a horse. After his escape, he went to the Yucatán, where he attempted to enlist the support of family members in getting him to Europe, where he planned to beg mercy from the pope. His brother-in-law in Mérida, however, fearing for his own liberty, denounced Cabello to the Franciscan provincial. Cabello was not seen again until May 1579 in Campeche, where he was apprehended while attempting to board a boat to Veracruz in lay clothing. He was eventually sent back to Mexico City, where he arrived on August 31, 1579. He was jailed again and a new trial ensued, but Cabello was able to escape from house arrest on August 11, 1580. He was next found in Jalapa playing cards on September 1. The guardian of the Franciscan house apprehended him and clapped him in irons, but the improvised cell was not nearly enough to hold a seasoned escape artist like Cabello, who slipped out the window and headed for the port of Veracruz. On November 2, 1580, attempting to board a ship headed for Spain, he was detained, arrested, and sent to Mexico City under armed guard.

At this point the Franciscan provincial and authorities asked the Inquisition to banish Cabello from Mexico and remit the entire case to the General Spanish Inquisition in Madrid. The Mexican inquisitors acceded and on January 27, 1581, ordered Cabello to be conducted to Spain. At this point the trail runs cold and we are left to speculate on Fray Alonso's fate.

The document that follows comes from the 1578 Inquisition trial against Cabello. It is a combination of a formal, written sermon combined with some notes and theological citations. It can be found

---

11.   By law any book lacking a title page was prohibited.

in the Archivo General de la Nación in Mexico in the Inquisition section, volume 88, expediente 1. Most of the sermon is in Spanish, though some sections are in Latin. The sermon first appeared in print as a transcription and partial translation (of the Latin portions into Spanish) in Martin Nesvig, "El sermón de un erasmista olvidado," *Boletín del Archivo General de la Nación* [Mexico] 6, no. 5 (2004).

The sermon puts on display the thought processes of a young man struggling to make sense of various ideas. It is not a brilliant piece, and it appears that Cabello was not a very good student of grammar or Erasmus, but it is an excellent example of an ordinary person trying to make sense of some of the major intellectual trends of his day.

In the translation that follows, I have attempted to make the sermon relatively comprehensible. In some ways this is a disservice to the prose, but in the end I decided in the interests of readability to correct some of Cabello's faulty Latin grammar and overly tortured Spanish. The reader will still find the piece a bit opaque and, at times, illogical or simply unclear. Nevertheless, there are moments when a real sense of spiritual fervor comes through and Cabello's affinity for Christocentric and internal, stripped-down, and simple devotion shine. The deliberate noncapitalization of the word for God, *dios*, is not a typo—Cabello clearly intended this, as he consistently capitalizes proper names beginning with the letter D, but not *dios*, or the Latin *deus*. This seems to reflect his discussion of the ineffable and mysterious, of the metaphysical meaning of the making of God into man through the birth of Jesus.

Two things make Cabello's sermon difficult. First, the subject is complicated and wrought with metaphysical subtleties. Ostensibly the theme is the Nativity of Jesus and the relationship of Christ's humanity with his divinity. The sermon draws on Paul's Letter to the Galatians, in which Paul debated new Christians in what is today Turkey. Among the issues facing Paul was the insistence by the Galatians on observing certain aspects of the Hebraic Law—circumcision in particular—while having become Christian converts. There are parallels—though Cabello was unaware of them because Castro's piece was never published—between the debate in Galatians, Cabello's sermon, and Castro's discussion of the conversion and education of the Indians. Castro was explicitly concerned with the theme of Galatians—to what extent should the old customs (whether of the pagans, the Jews, or the Indians) be tolerated in the process of conversion? Should new Christians be allowed full and equal membership in the Church? To what extent should new Christians be tainted by their association with Jewish, pagan, or Indian custom and belief?

Cabello's discussion, however, seems to largely abandon these issues of conversion for a more purely spiritual and metaphysical contemplation of Christ's humanity and the New Law. For Cabello the issue is how God can demean himself by making himself into a sinful creature—namely, human. Cabello never really answers his own question. But he offers some suggestions about his views. He seems to have been working through a Christological spirituality— a very Christ-centered view of Catholicism, which, by definition, would denigrate the cult of the saints and Marianism, quite in keeping with his Erasmian sympathies. For Cabello, the making of God into humanity, through the birth of Christ, was an unfathomable miracle and insult. This seems to reveal a pessimistic view of humanity, which should not be surprising since Cabello had only recently been humiliated by his own confreres and the Inquisition.

Secondly, the sermon is difficult because it is, frankly, poorly written. His Spanish is grotesquely overburdened with attempts at grandeur, often leading to near unintelligibility. Yet at times he seems like a real idealist, a young man caught up in the excitement of Erasmus's criticisms of the Church and of mendicant orders. Cabello also offers an extended contemplation of Bonaventure's view of spirituality as diffuse and all-encompassing. He quotes Aquinas at length, perhaps attempting to demonstrate that he had been studying hard in his cell. Works by mainstream Dominican theologians like Vitoria were found there. But his citation of authorities is often either incorrect or incomprehensible. In the end the thoughts of a young man convicted of heresy, conflicted about his role in the Franciscan order, and frustrated by the quashing of his curiosity about Erasmus, are laid bare in their all too human way by his pen.

In making this sermon available here, it was necessary to deviate from both literal translation and linear transcription. As mentioned, Cabello's style is often florid and jumbled, rambling, and even somewhat difficult to understand. Likewise, the sermon manuscript contains dozens, if not hundreds, of abbreviations—both normal stylistic abbreviations typical of mid-sixteenth-century paleography as well as abbreviations for the citation of theological authorities like

Aquinas, Augustine, and others. In addition, as the sermon represents more his own notes for a public presentation than a formal written essay, certain norms of abbreviation are sometimes omitted in the original. In the interests of readability I have spelled out abbreviated words and names. In Cabello's time it was common in both manuscript and printed material for theologians and canon lawyers to draw on standard, well-known texts, like Aquinas's *Summa theologiae*, without providing specific citations or, in some cases, even the name of the author or title of the work. Accordingly, I have provided citations where there are none in the original.

Alonso Cabello
"Sermon on the Nativity of Our Lord"
(Cholula, December [24?], 1577)

For our very reverend father and religious audience:

Part in which I discuss that which is known about the free method of proceeding little by little.[12] Whoever wishes to speak of the subject which this blessed time presents us must speak of the greatest act, the work most full of mysteries, marvels, divine power, wisdom, and mercy of all that have been told. Whoever wishes to fix one's gaze on the devout and solemn meaning of these days must fix his gaze on that which cannot be perfectly understood by men, nor explained by the language or wit of angels. Thus, if we were given the new law in this chapter, whose meaning is usually entrusted to masters and the world's philosophers to explain, then it would seem that there would be no reason for us to speak or think or arrogantly waste words to no good end or purpose.

What does it mean for god to make himself into man?[13] What could it mean to present himself to us on this most blessed night in a manger, surrounded by animals, shedding tears, emitting sobs, and issuing whimpers? Would could it mean that a god so powerful, a god so pure, a god so holy, a god so free, a god unto himself, who has

12.   The original Latin reads, "pars in quem ductio qua[e]dam, in qua era peratur emplitudo, ex qui noti, expresori liber mod[us] pedetentim procedendi." Cabello's text contains numerous grammatical corruptions, which I have cleaned up in my translation.
13.   Here, as in other places, Cabello does not capitalize the word for God, *deus*.

absolutely no need of anything beyond himself, by his own nature and serendipitous virtue would voluntarily imbue such a vile, low creature with all his gifts, a creature so weak, so impure, so iniquitous and evil, so captive to evil, so despoiled of all true beauty, so needy and lacking of all good? Why would he deliver this creature and give it access to the throne of his godliness, to the union of his person, to the enjoyment of his good fortune, to the communion of his grandeur, to the familiarity of his secret, and to the honor of his monarchy? How could the same equanimity and justice also forget such a horrible and grave offense as the blind, ungrateful nature of the pathetic man which he made? To abandon the rigor of the laws, and to ignore the eternal and most grave majesty, having treated himself with cruelty, rudeness, immoderation, so that he attaches to this fool a civil, pleasing, and polite creature?

One thing has, is, and will always characterize the eternal knowledge of god: his superabundant awareness, his highest valor, his most admirable majesty and greatness, which contrasts with our immense lack of merit and lowness. These are the two hinges of the secret of all the eternal wisdom of our sovereign lord created of his own knowledge and of the knowledge of that which lies beyond. Beyond this there is nothing which needs to be known, or comprehended, nor is there anything which falls beneath some object of wisdom, because under this category are subsumed those things which are created as well as those which can be raised for this purpose.

And as god is holy and pure his divine understanding is forever tied to these two things. And wherever our lord turns his eyes, what does he find regarding us, creatures which he created from nothing, if not a call for justice? If he looked, would he not see such an ineffable power offended, injured, and despised? What did justice say here? "Ah! I will take vengeance on my foes and fully repay my enemies." [14] If he looked at man, he found a void full of pride, unappreciative of divine majesty, surrounded by impurity. The offense to you was lamentable and doubled by yet another. It was a soul neglectful of its need for correction, swaddled and bound up with all those things which are hateful and abhorrent to his divine gaze. What did justice say then? "All who forsake you shall be in disgrace; the rebels in the land shall be put to shame." [15] What would come to pass in the secret

14. In the margin: Isaiah 1:24.
15. In the margin: Jeremiah 17[:13].

which is divine judgment? Who then would advocate so intimately for the miserable creature of humanity? What other words would the ineffable verb pronounce if not those which his prophet utters to the same end: ["]Why should I pardon you these things?["][16] For god comes and not only does he avert his gaze from our worthlessness, he also makes note of everything that he values, man was from him, and he looks this way as if everything in him enticed him to forgive us. Using his divine liberality, beneficence, and nobility, he is not content to make god into man and give him everything he could. And his might, seing the breadth of human capacity, he could not extend or receive any more than this. What then does this mean? Who can speak of this and give cause? Whose tongue is not rendered mute? Whose heart does not marvel? O the depth of the riches both of the wisdom and knowledge of god! "How inscrutable are his judgments and how unsearchable his ways!"[17]

Accordingly, in this matter we must now say of ourselves that which is said of the comedian: "Seek not the things that are too high for thee, and search not into things above thy ability."[18] "And let us not be overly curious, because he who scrutinizes His majesty will be oppressed by his glory."[19] Let us be content with that which he would give us in order to be rooted in the firmest faith, because that is what suffices for our understanding and which subjects and humiliates all human reason.[20]

Part Two: Where we arrive at the description of the birth of our lord christ. Let us marvel, then, and wonder, because today, on such a day as this, the words of the holy scripture, the admonitions of the

16. Jeremiah 5:7.

17. In the margin: Romans 8 [i.e., 11:33].

18. Ecclesiasticus 3:22. Douay-Rheims translation.

19. Proverbs 25:27. The Latin Cabello employs reads, "qui scrutator est maiestatis, opprimetur a Gloria" (*opprimetur* is apparently a late medieval or Hispanicized spelling of *opprimitur*, found in the Vulgate). My translation differs from modern English ones in an attempt to capture the flavor of Cabello's version.

20. Cabello may be following Bonaventure's commentaries on Lombard here. In qu. 2, ar. 2 of the foreword to the *Questions*, Bonaventure examines Lombard's discussion first of Proverbs 25:27 and then, in qu. 2, ar. 3, discusses Ecclesiasticus 3:21. As was often the case, Cabello's comprehension of his studies was less than perfect, as his paraphrase of Ecclesiasticus 3:21–23 is terrible at best. The rest of the passage to which he alludes, and which would have been familiar to his Franciscan audience, is "Be not curious in unnecessary matters: for more things are shewed unto thee than men understand. For many are deceived by their own vain opinion; and an evil suspicion hath overthrown their judgment."

faith, and the purest ceremonies of the holy church illuminate our gaze with a supernatural knowledge of a strange figure never before seen or heard of or considered in previous centuries. In the deep silence of a tranquil night, in a poor hovel, a tender virgin—even in her external appearance full of a celestial innocence, honesty, and beauty—knelt before a recently born infant, who had just been born of her, without showing sign of childbirth. And he swathed in poor swaddling atop hay in a manger, shivering from cold and crying. Two creatures with miraculous understanding in front of the manger full of new fear and reverence. A venerable man, with complete gravity and holiness, seated in the same way, revering the child.

Angelic songs, an assembly of shepherds, and finally in all things, in every nook and cranny among those creatures, by that bell, an unknowable celestial melody and joy, by which we are accustomed to feel jubilation: and other things, which pious hearts contemplate and feel other sentiments. Let us now bring forth a religious heart before this spectacle, believing faithfully that that child is god himself made flesh, and that the virgin is his mother, and that ancient and honored man his nourishment, and those angels his ministers, those beasts his witnesses, those shepherds, his worshippers and sacrificers, and finally, that poor doorway, the house of his royal majesty and glory. What will he think here? What will he say here? What will he contemplate here? How will he proceed? What documents will he consider? What will he feel? Truly this is that place and time in which the apostle warns faithful souls with those profound words: "For this reason I kneel before the father [of our lord Jesus christ] . . . that christ may dwell in your hearts through faith; that you, rooted and grounded in love, may have strength to comprehend with all the holy ones what is the breadth and length and height and depth."[21]

Indeed, here, here are confirmed these mysterious words, here resides the breadth of divine charity, here the depth of his mercy, here the sublimity of his judgment, here the profundity of his humility, here the generosity and civility for sinners. Here one sees the height of his divine mysteries, here all the power of divine manifestation, here one learns of his greatness, here his kindness, here his mercy, here his love, here his desire for our welfare, here, finally, the pure gaze, clean and free of all false opinion, and of the affection

---

21. In the margin: In Ephesians 3[:14, 17–18]. Here, as in other places, Cabello capitalizes "Jesus," as a proper name, but not "Christ," just as he does not capitalize *dios* (God).

nearly shown by the condition of the divine nature, and the miracle of its qualities, its inner thoughts and conceptions.

It seems that our good lord did not want to leave anything about himself hidden from mortals. He wanted to give us everything, he wanted to show us everything, he wanted to bring out everything from the highest secret of his home, so that he could see it discussed, felt, communicated in this world. Where goes a voice without meaning? What shall I say? What end do I presume to find in the abyss of infinity? Where will I go blindly without a guide? For as the soul learns beside me the lesson of this mystery, let us begin with the first letters of this book. Let us extend our sight to what was, what came to pass in his substance, and on that which preceded him and that which followed him. Let us not be content with any old master, but rather let us seek shelter in that great apostle Paul, the secretary, council servant, notary of these causes, the master of these doctrines. In a full and gracious style, keeping an admirable order, Paul proposes to us in the lesson everything which is licit for mortals to consider and everything to which they can extend their lance, and let fly one's heart: "when the fullness of time had come."[22]

You see here, my fathers, the order and procession of this mystery and of our sermon. There is nothing more to see here than each word of this lesson in itself: ["]god sent his son, born of a woman, born under the law, to ransom those under the law.["][23] Every point of doctrine proceeds by its circumstances, and the circumstances of this subject are those that the apostle relates here, because in the consideration of each word one sees the grandeur of the benefaction. Who sent? god.[24] Whom did he send? His son. How did he send him? Made flesh and born of a woman. In what state? In keeping with and subject to the law. Why did he send? To redeem and save the lost who could not be saved by their law alone. The extent of this argument will be resolved, then, in three points, so that we do not proceed without order. Who sent and who was sent? How? Why?

From these premises will we interpret correctly because what is inferred is that we love, and who has treated us so well? What is it if not that which united us with the purest and most devout charity to

---

22. Galatians 4:4.
23. Galatians 4:4–5.
24. Even though *dios* is the first word in the sentence, Cabello, in keeping with his practice, does not capitalize it.

the spirit, with whom we were directed in that singular nature of the union of spirit and person? What is it, but that we are pleased with saintly customs and a life of arduous study to please him? What is it, but that we reject immensely the sin that our lover and redeemer infinitely abhorred, and because of that loathing put himself through frauds and labors?

This is the exchange which god wants from our soul as a reward for such an illustrious and absolute benefit. Because although we are indebted entirely to a god, he did not want to proclaim us debtors until he showed us openly the reason for captivating us with such a tremendous and excessive obligation, because we would owe him and would have to pay with obedience. You see here the loving signs that god gave us from his ancient love. It was not to provide for us some new love that he did not have for us before, because we never gave any reason for new love. That love has always existed and has been eternally with god, because it was nothing except out of pure kindness and mercy. Today's work was a declaration of that infinite love which since eternity has been sealed in the divine heart.

And in order that we may see him and know him, and not doubt him, he has today made a great entrance, he has impetuously manifested himself, as much as he could. If he were not god, such would not have been made manifest, because this effect is from that cause and that cause from that effect. And for this effect another cause is not necessary, and from such a cause one could not expect a lesser effect.

As relates to the first point, then, it is of utmost importance to consider the nature and condition of the benefactor, since no creature would dare so unless he entices us by his will: "Come over to me, all ye that desire me, and be filled with my fruits."[25] And that man [presumably Solomon] full of god himself thus spoke so truthfully: "For to know thee is perfect justice: and to know thy justice, and thy power, is the root of immortality."[26] And although this science and knowledge is quite necessary, it is also very difficult, as Saint Bernard explains with vivid feeling: "Who is this who is so ordinary in words but so distant in action? In the same way that we speak words, in his recondite majesty his affection baffles our internal vision."[27]

25. In the margin: Ecclesiasticus 24[:26]. Douay-Rheims translation.

26. In the margin: Wisdom of Solomon 15[:3]. Douay-Rheims translation. In the margin below: Also Lamentations 3[:25]: "Good is the lord to one who waits for him, to the soul that seeks him."

27. In the margin: "Bernard[us] de Esoc. 5." It is not clear to which work this refers.

Part Three: In which we come to the knowledge of the great benefaction.[28] If in order to be able to discover something of such profundity we had not been given such an important reading today, who
would have spoken of it? Plato investigated it, Aristotle investigated
it, Socrates investigated it, and many others did as well, but all their
work was empty because they did not hear the wails of this child who
while crying instructs us from the pulpit of his cradle. Saint Bernard
refers to god in the same voice and words which we use to speak of
ourselves and which we use to speak of him. He thus inflates the
truth of his common and vernacular truth in his work. We say that
we are ourselves and we say that god is himself: that we love, that god
loves. That we understand, and that god understands. That we live and
that god lives. But do we see the same meaning? In no way. God loves
with charity. He knows with truth. He judges with justice. He imag-
ines with majesty. He rules as prince. He defends as health. He works
as virtue. He reveals as lights. He is present as piety. He understands
as wisdom. He lives as life. He is as the being itself, root of all being.
Etc. According to Dionysius and the other theologians, our concrete
ideas are improper and our abstract ones more accurate in explaining
divine qualities, though some explanations are left undefended. To
call god alive, good, just, holy, powerful, and merciful is improper. To
call him life, goodness, justice, sanctity, power, and mercy is truth. For
there is thus a difference in the character of those attributes in god
and in man, just as there is a distinction between the nature of those
in the abstract in god and that of the same virtues considered in the
adequate and vulgar meaning of those words. For it is important to
note that between god and his creatures there is a certain similitude
and that in all of them there is a vestige of divine nature and that
there is nothing in his creatures which could not be found, but in per-
fected form, in their creator, since he is the beginning of all existence,
conditions, and perfections.[29] Thus the nature of our understanding,
capable as it is of divine light, which, when concerning the science
of creation, rises easily to the knowledge of the eternal given certain
circumstances which, for the moment, we will not discuss. Consequently, these same voices with which created beings vaguely make
themselves known, through this path a motive will be given, and

28. This section contains various grammatical corruptions, which I have corrected.
29. In the margin: Saint Bonaventure, *On the Mind's Journey to God* [*In itinerarium mentis in Deum*].

they will help us approach the secret knowledge of the creator, who by no words can be made understandable, he does not embody all the imperfection and crassness that these words imply.

Bernard then asks: who is god? And he responds that "nothing better occurs to me than the response he received to that question: I am who I am."[30] And this with great reason, because there is nothing more consistent with eternity than god himself. All his attributes are resolved and understood in this: he is. What else is god? He is that without which nothing exists. Thus nothing can exist without him, just as he cannot exist without himself. What is god? "What I told you from the beginning."[31] Origin, root, source, beginning of everything substantial or accidental. What is god? God is an eternity, an immutable being, a constant actual nature, from whom the centuries can neither quit nor add, for whom nothing was coeternal. What is god? "Of him, and through him, and to him, are all things."[32] Out of him everything by creation. In him everything as in preserved vigor and vivifying origin. Through him everything as in a sole author, and accidentally to all those things directed. For if everything is in him, where is he? One can say nothing less. Where does he take charge? Pious questions—where is he not? I will hardly say, because where is god not present? God is incomprehensible.

But with all this, he who has fully reached what he knows, that he is not enclosed in any place, he is everywhere and he is excluded from no location in his certain and incomprehensible way. Thus as all places are in him, he is in all of them. One of the evangelists says, "He was in the world."[33] But where was he before there was a world? Where he was then, he is now, and where he is now, he was then. Thus there is nothing beyond him and consequently he is in himself.

30. In the margin: Exodus 2. It is, rather, Exodus 3:14, which in the Latin Bible reads, "Dixit Deus ad Moysen: EGO SUM QUI SUM. Ait: Sic dices filiis Israel; QUI EST, misit me ad vos," and in the English translation, "God replied, 'I am who am.' Then he added, 'This is what you shall tell the Israelites: I AM sent me to you.'" The original Hebrew is "Yhwh asher Yhwh," though this implies future tense, "I will be what I will be," which implies ineffability, eternity, and boundlessness. I am thankful to Emily Michelson for her help with this famous discussion on the naming of the Old Testament God.

31. In the margin: John 8[:25].

32. In the margin: Romans 11[:36]. Cabello writes "Ex quo o[mn]ia, in quo omnia, per quem omnia," which is a paraphrase of "Quoniam ex ipso, et per ipsum, et in ipso sunt omnia" (For from him and through him and for him are all things).

33. In the margin: John 1[:10].

What else is god? Something for which no equal or better can be imagined. What is god? Pure and spiritual simplicity, in whom there can be no division of parts, nor circumscription of attributes, nor diversity of quality, nor composition, nor anything else in him that is not simple, pure, individual, that simplest essence itself that is god. He is pure, he is simple, he is perfect, he is constant, he is always present. From him nothing is withdrawn or forgotten, nothing of this world that is not of the places, times, and things that he himself ineffably created and that are united with him. Nothing of his substance is distributed in them. Nothing of god is divided, nothing of god is united to something else, because he is one, not united. He is not a unity of parts like a body. He is not distracted with effects like a soul. He is not subject to accidents like living creatures. May the same god of unity and the perfect trinity protect me. Is it for fear of uttering so much, or using many words, that we exceed ourselves or say that he is more than he is? No! For we take advantage of him a great deal, and though we desire much, we are always left to walk in the same field.

How can we exaggerate this unity if he himself is not the trinity? It is certain. Later do we destroy that which we have said of the one? No! First let us confirm this admirable unity, in which three are one, father, son, and holy spirit, which we confess as one, one god, one nature, one essence, one power, one knowledge, one will, one understanding, one love, etc. In order to prove that god is one, one could have used reasons taken in part from natural philosophy. But arriving at this point regarding the three, comes that strongest reason of the catholic faith, and that alone proves it and that alone is enough for me. There is no other, no do I desire another, because even though another might exist, nothing proves it better than faith. But what is this number without number? If he is one, where is the number? As that one substance is three persons, who will deny the number, because in truth there are three? He who began to count will tell you that those three persons are one substance? To scrutinize this is temerity, to believe it, piety, to know it and love it, life and eternal life.

O most beautiful spirit, O supreme emperor and judge of the universe, will you illuminate our spirit, clarify our understanding, light and embrace our will so that the spirit will correct this entire deviation and vanity of words and enclose it in the secret spiritual love and knowledge of your greatness? Will I say that you are my god? What will I call you? How will I consider you? You are omnipotent; you are the most benevolent virtue. You are eternal flame. You are incommutable reason. You are the highest beatitude. You create minds to participate with you. You animate them so they are sentient. You inspire them so that they may appeal to you. You open them so that they receive you. You absolve them so that they merit you. You inflame them so that they are zealous. You fertilize them so that they multiply. You set them right so that they do good. You inform them for benevolence and you moderate them for wisdom. You straighten them for virtue. You visit them for consolation. You illuminate them for knowledge. You perpetuate them for immortality. You compliment them for happiness. You surround them for security. O glory of the humble, affliction for the perverse. O grandeur, O breadth, O width, O majesty, O unthinkable, intangible, uninvestigable length. O hatred of sin, O detester of evil and what is evil. O incommutable impartiality, O brave justice you are the sign of all good, you are all power, you are all worth.[34]

Part Four: In which it is discussed why god sent forth his son, born of a woman. "God sent his son, born of a woman, born under the law."[35] By a strange consequence of the marvelous power of our great god, where will we stop? Did he punish man? Did he condemn man? Did he loathe man? Did he annihilate man? Did he cast man far from himself? No, no, no. He sent his son, etc. He sent his own son in order to redeem man. Who is this man? What did this man deserve? Is that he who was created in god's image and likeness, adorned by sovereign gifts and riches, placed in the paradise of delights, certified by eternal well-being, loved of god, accompanied by angels, honored and revered by all creatures, but then raised his hand against god, spat in his face, rejected his gifts, closed his ears and left him speechless and tried to make away with his kingdom? That is man himself, and no other. Is it he who worshipped idols, who wasted himself at every chance, who knew he offended his creator, who desired everything that he should not, and despised everything that god loved, and transgressed everything that he ordered? Mankind itself. Considering everything god has done, how has he punished him? Where has

34. This paragraph is a loose rendering of Bonaventure's work "The Five Feasts of the Child Jesus." See "Las cinco festividades del niño Jesús," in *Obras de San Buenaventura*, ed. Fr. León Amorós, Bernardo Apperibay, and Miguel Oromi (Madrid: Biblioteca de Autores Cristianos, 1962), 2:359–89.

35. Galatians 4:4.

he placed him? Just how far with ferocity and furor has he debased him? He sent his son, etc.

He sent his son today, today made and born of a woman, subjected his son today to the law, so that he could redeem mankind and take away the sin of the world which he [man] iniquitously incurred by his own will. This message that god made of his son today is represented for us because this is the tender child who today is held in the arms of the sweet mother and placed on the rough manger and cries. This is the child born god and man in a person, and in the end although you see him so humiliated in this way, and in such circumstances as to cause spasms and ecstasy—know that he comes quite ordered, composed, and ready for that which the eternal father sent him. "They name him wonder-counselor, god-hero, father-forever, prince of peace. His dominion is vast and forever peaceful, from David's throne, and over his kingdom, which he confirms and sustains by judgment and justice, both now and forever."[36] But what force moved god to give us his own son in such a form? Was it not posible that as he loves us so much he could have done it in another way? Certainly he could have redeemed us in a thousand other ways.

But in the end he is god and all his works are of god, and in nothing is he shown diminished, for where it matters most and is demonstrated most amply is in his will and determination to redeem us from sin. He wanted this work, the greatest of those which he has created, and in which he is best seen, to be the most perfect posible and most appropriate to its goal.[37] ["]Hence Saint Augustine says in book 13, chapter 10 of *De trinitate:* 'We shall also show that other ways were not wanting to god, to whose power all things are equally subject; but that there was not a more fitting way of healing our misery.'["] In order to further the goodness of man, ["]first, with regard to faith, which is made more certain by believing god

36. Isaiah 9:6–7.
37. Quoted from Aquinas, *Summa theologiae* 3.1.2. Much of the following is quoted from the same passage. Cabello does not provide quotation marks here since his audience would have been familiar with Aquinas and later he notes the citation. Since he is providing a Spanish vernacular discussion of a text that at that time was only available in Latin, he makes some minor deviations. Even in quoting Aquinas and Augustine, Cabello never capitalizes the word "God," even though he capitalizes Aquinas, Augustine, Leo, and other names. The translations in the text from *Summa theologiae* are based on the 1912– 25 translation by the Fathers of the English Dominican Province, which can be found at http://www.ccel.org/ccel/aquinas/summa.i.html.

himself who speaks; hence Saint Augustine says in book 11, chapter 2 of *de civit[ate] dei*: 'In order that man might journey more trustfully toward the truth, the truth itself, the son of god, having assumed human nature, established and founded faith.' . . . [W]ith regard to hope, which is thereby greatly strengthened; hence Augustine says 13 *de trinit[ate]*: 'Nothing was so necessary for raising our hope as to show us how deeply god loved us. And what could afford us a stronger proof of this than that the son of god should become a partner with us of human nature?' . . . With regard to charity, which is greatly enkindled by this [breath]; hence Augustine says in *de cathechizan[dis] rudib[us]* [chapter 4]: 'What greater cause is there of the Lord's coming that to show god's love for us?' And he afterwards adds: 'If we have been slow to love, at least let us hasten to love in return.'["]

["]With regard to well-doing["] and the observance of the divine law, ["]in which he set us an example; hence Augustine says in a sermon (xxii *de Temp.*): 'Man who might be seen was not to be followed; but god was to be followed, who could not be seen. And therefore god was made man, that he who might be seen by man, and whom man might follow, might be shown to man.' . . . With regard to the full participation of the divinity, which is the true bliss of man and end of human life["] which was given to us righteously by the incarnation and this appears to be its principal cause, and was the purpose of what the same saint [i.e., Augustine] ["]says in a sermon (xiii *de Temp.*): 'god was made man, that man might be made god.'["]

What will we say, then, of these pertinent antidotes that god created for us in order to cleanse us of sin and deliver us from evil. [Paraphrasing Aquinas] Will man prefer the devil and his persuasions, seeing god palpably before his eyes? Who will sully the dignity of human nature?

["]And Saint Pope Leo says in a sermon on [this festival] [*De Nativitate* xxi]: 'Learn, man, your worth; and being made a partner of the divine nature, refuse to return by evil deeds to your former worthlessness."[38] ["In order to do away with man's presumption, the grace of god is commended, though no merits of ours went before [as Augustine says (*De Trin.* xiii, 17)]." Also ["]'man's pride, which is the

---

38. "Learn, man": Cabello elides the word Christian as quoted by Aquinas ("Learn, O Christian").

greatest stumbling-block to our clinging to god, can be convinced and cured by humility so great,' as Augustine says [in the same place].["] For in order to liberate man by juridical means from the burden of sin, divine counsel was god made man and man, in that same nature, fell and had to be saved. ["]For a mere man could not have done this, and god did not owe it; hence it behooved him to be both god and man.["] [Paraphrasing Aquinas] It behooved god to become man in order to provide so many other tools that go beyond our understanding which came from this incarnation. All of this is the doctrine of Saint Thomas, part 3, question 1, article 2: that is, made from woman, made man.

This point opened for us the widest area of questions and considerations concerning the incarnation, but there is not enough time, nor would they even by chance be well received considering our current spiritual state: let us consider then that doctrinal word: made under the law. The interlineal gloss accedes: Not so that he himself was purified by the law but that he purify those who were subjected to the law. That the son of god, subjected to the law, came is something which should motivate our admiration on seeing god made man. On two points the mystery of the incarnation of god is resolved: in having made himself man for us and in having subjected himself to the law for us. Doubtless those are the points which shock me or in which the providence of divine wisdom should be praised the most.

This subjection of god to the law is the perfection of his holiest incarnation, and with this god concluded all the parts of this work. Moreover there were two laws to which god subjected himself for us. One of these was the divine sentence which god imposed on us after the sin of Adam in Genesis 3[:17]: "Cursed be the ground because of you! In toil shall you eat its yield, etc." Do you wish to see it? Note the time, place, and company in which he is born. Look at the gifts and shelter he has. Contemplate him if you are not insensitive, and you will not be hardened; contemplate him shriveled by the cold, and the harsh conditions which clamorously befall his delicate flesh. Contemplate him among beasts. Contemplate him abandoned of every favor save that which that chosen virgin gave him with every consideration and diligence.

But it seems to me that god purposefully wanted to afflict us in order to captivate us, for if here one does not imagine a secret providence and divine wisdom, I must marvel at seeing such a son relinquished from the arms of such a mother that no pain impeded, and reclined in such a repulsive bed, in a vile manger, on a hard floor, and in a terrible cold, at the maw of beasts. This was not negligence on the part of that maiden, at whose beauty the sun, moon, and stars marvel. This was not neglience on her part, who had such abundant love for her son that it was truly recorded in Luke 2[:35]: "and you yourself a soul will pierce." Rather it was verification of the words "made under the law." And of the words said much earlier: "Yet it was our infirmities that he bore, our sufferings that he endured."[39] He wanted to subject him to the law of suffering so that he would understand the task given him. Thence we extract a grave document of patience in the works and penalties which we suffer for our sin, which is fundamental for the exercise of all virtue and purification of the soul in order to see god. There must be something in this, since Jesus christ voluntarily assumed these tasks and suffered them, which he would not have done unless it was of great importance for us.

It seems that if god intended to come to us in person to redeem us, it was with the desire that we guard his law, to which he wanted to entrust everything possible to men. Nevertheless, "thus it is fitting for us to fulfill all righteousness."[40] The other law was that of Moses, and to this also he was subjected as we see clearly eight days from today.[41] O christian, o friar redeemed by the blood of this child that here and now see the profession of his imitation, life, and virtue, if by chance you are not who you should be, if you are wicked, if you prevaricate in your vows, with what shame, with what kind of countenance do you hear these words? Are you not confused? Do you not tremble? In what esteem do you hold that the son of god was subjected to the law for your sake? Do you suppose that he wanted *you* to subject *yourself* to the law for him? That *you* keep the law for *him*? That *you* obey his law? That *you* lower *your* neck for the yoke of his law?[42] Oh, how terrible and monstrous that we believe this and examine this—and I am the first to commit such an error—that we view it as a duty, if not to say a mockery.

39. In the margin: Isaiah 53[:4]
40. In the margin: Matthew 3[:15].
41. Referring to the Hebraic law of circumcision. See Luke 2:21: "And when eight days were accomplished for the circumcising of the child, his name was called Jesus."
42. Referring again to Bonaventure.

If our heart is moved to these things, although said by my unworthy and contemptible mouth, what class does our faith have? How much do we believe? It must not even be a grain of mustard, because I hold it as impossible that the truly faithful, who has the faith planted alive in his heart, that he not do these things with great feeling.

God was made man from the law and subject to the law! Oh, how much our obedience and observance of the law must please god. How he must desire and long for us to obey the law! What did he not do, no stone left unmoved, nothing left untried, in order to attract us to this subjection. I do not want to deal with punishment, which seems evident.[43] No, not of pain or hell, it is not with this that god sought to have us love and come closer to him. From this child subjected to the law, this image, I propose that the noble heart be captivated by love and charity. This, this, this is enough in order not to confuse and confound. God made man subject to the law. Oh, who would have the spirit and words in order to extol this. Forgive me, fathers, for having taken in my hands something I cannot resolve. Every one of you must endure even more than what I say, as our sins must be felt so deeply.

Of one thing I am quite convinced and I believe it without doubt, that in this world there is no visible state closer and similar to the image and to the imitation of christ than ours. Likewise in this world there is no heart which carries it along perfectly, as only a needle holds it captive to the interests of this world. I have experience and knowledge in this. This most blessed rule wants hearts to be free, men naked like this child. That maker of Jesus christ, that second Jesus christ, that evangelical patriarch, our seraphic father Saint Francis, did not create, did not form a religion so that people would suffer. This is what god gave his spirit to feel, a remnant of peace, and the truth said by the prophet. He felt that the creature had to atone for god having been subjected to the law.

Not us—because the love we have for virtue, for our rule is so superficial that minute instances of some necessity or opinion cause us to destroy that rule at every step. I do not want to break my rule,

43. In the margin: John 1. The relationship between these lines and the Gospel of John is not explicit. John discusses God made man and the relationship between Christ and the Old Law, treated above by Cabello. Cf. John 1:14: "And the Word became flesh"; John 1:17: "because while the law was given through Moses, grace and truth came through Jesus Christ."

but sometimes, away from the friary, I want to say—forget it! And then I want to ride on horseback, and then I want to break the fast. What is worse is that poverty being the fundamental principal, decoration, and ornament of our sacred religion, in few words, with little imagination, with some petty words with I don't know what false pretenses and smelling of I don't know what appearances, I puff up my own purse. Even if these things were necessary and their cause true, without being extreme, it is the case that love for religion, the rule, and apostolic state has a short root; may god remedy my state.

It only remains to say about that word in order that it redeem those who err beneath the law, that god made flesh gives us great profit, and he created many great benefits for us. This spurs the memory to these doctrines of Saint Paul: "And you who once were alienated and hostile in mind because of evil deeds he has now reconciled in his fleshly body through his death, to present you holy, without blemish, and irreproachable before him."[44]

The Figure of Ezekiel

"And I saw and behold in the firmament etc."[45] Then I looked in the firmament that was above the head of the cherubims and there appeared over them as it were a sapphire stone, or the appearance of the sun, and he said to a cherubim: it is wisdom. The firmament represents the determination and will to redeem the creature. He was above the wisdom of god because in a certain way it was against the order which ordinary wisdom of god concerning that which should be above man. The sapphire represents the mercy which was the foundation of this work. At the time of the incarnation a kind of sun appeared above this sapphire because it represented the fulfillment in the plenitude of time. The divine will arrived at the actual moment of incarnation, and this sun was christ. It is said that he was not perfect because he did not appear in full force and divine splendor, and even though he shed light on the world like a sun of justice, not everyone knew him.

44. In the margin: Letter to the Colossians 1[:21–22]
45. Ezekiel 10:1. The passages from Ezekiel that follow are given here in the Douay-Rheims translation. Cabello does not cite these passages, but he does provide a loose Spanish rendering of the scriptural Latin in his sermon notes.

"He spoke to the man, that was clothed with linen."[46] This would represent the work of christ by words which explain how eternal counsel was given in redemption and which had to be fulfilled by christ in his humanity, even by virtue of his divinity. And thus humanity is represented by the man dressed in linen. "Come in between the wheels, under the cherub, and fill the hollow of thy hands with coals of fire from between the cherubim, and scatter them over the city."[47]

"Who has blessed us in christ with every spiritual blessing in the heavens."[48]

"You are the most handsome of men; fair speech has graced [your lips]."[49]

"And he went in in my sight. And the cherubims stood on the right side of the house, when the man went in, and a cloud filled the inner court."[50] The Jews admired this because they were in the inner court of god. "And the glory of the lord was lifted up from above the cherub to the threshold of the house: and the house was filled with the cloud, and the court was filled with the brightness of the glory of the lord."[51] "A veil lies over their hearts." [52]

---

46. Ezekiel 10:2.
47. Ibid.
48. In the margin: Ephesians [1:3].
49. In the margin: Psalm 24 [i.e., 45:3].
50. Ezekiel 10:2–3.
51. Ezekiel 10:4.
52. In the margin: 2 Corinthians 3[:15].

3

The Inquisitional Deputy on Witches

By 1588, Diego Muñoz had begun to act as the Inquisition's *comisa-*
rio. He would go on to be one of the most prolific, wide-ranging
comisarios of New Spain, sending hundreds upon hundreds of letters,
depositions, and investigations about suspicious religious activities
in rural Michoacán until his presumed death in 1626. The chronicler
Alonso de la Rea remarked, "His words were few but so sententious
and eloquent that today his writings are preserved as if they were
of a Justus Lipsius, as much for his narration as for the handwriting
since he was an excellent scribe."[1]

Celaya, where he recorded the denunciations of presumed
witchcraft reproduced here, was far afield of his normal area west
of Pátzcuaro, but the various demands on him as a well-respected
administrator meant that from time to time he traveled to Querétaro and Valladolid to attend to matters relating to the Franciscan
order. Muñoz was in Querétaro in September 1611 for the interim
provincial meeting of the Franciscans, but in October he was back
near Tancítaro-Uruapan, in Pirihuén.[2] In 1614 he was in Querétaro,
Acauato, and then, in the autumn, in Celaya.[3]

By 1614 the landscape of both the Franciscan mission and the
"frontiers" was shifting. The older period of intense idealistic evan-
gelization was over. Tlatelolco was a shadow of its former self. Horrifying plagues and demographic collapse had devastated the Indian
populations of central Mexico and Michoacán.[4] Churches were falling
down. Even the grand Franciscan convent in Valladolid, the capital of

1. Rea, *Chrónica,* fols. 95–96. Justus Lipsius was a Flemish humanist and the
royal historiographer for Philip II of Spain.

2. AGN, Inq., vol. 292, exp. s/n, fol. 150.

3. AGN, Inq., vol. 302.

4. For the case of Michoacán in particular, see Gonzalo Aguirre Beltrán, *Problemas*
de la población indígena de la Cuenca del Tepacaltepec, Memorias del Instituto Nacional
Indigenista, vol. 3 (Mexico City: Ediciones del Instituto Nacional Indigenista, 1952).

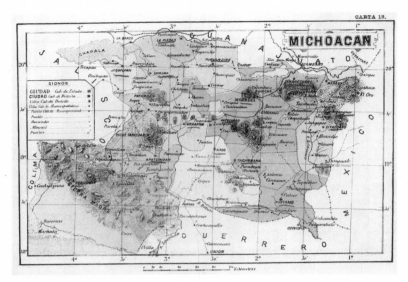

Fig. 4 Map of Michoacán. From Antonio García Cubas, *Atlas metódico para la enseñanza de la geografía de la Republica Mexicana* (1899). Courtesy the David Rumsey Map Collection.

Michoacán, was in such poor condition by 1615 because of decreased donations at the Mass and lack of general funding that the friars were obliged to beg the crown for thirty thousand pesos—a spectacular sum—for its repair.[5]

In the Bajío region, including Celaya, Spaniards were given land grants (*mercedes*) to populate the immediate frontier between the old Tarascan confederation, now demographically crumbling, and the nomadic Chichimec regions to the north, as a kind of bulwark of Spanish settlement as well as an incipient breadbasket for the now booming mines in Zacatecas and Guanajuato. Celaya was rapidly growing and had become a hotbed of denunciations of "witchcraft."[6]

In 1614, the inquisitors in Mexico asked Muñoz to act on their behalf in Celaya, which had no permanent *comisario* and in fact had never seen the Inquisition. On October 19, Muñoz delivered what was known as the edict of the faith, an exhortation to all citizens to

5. AGI México 28 n. 26.
6. For discussion of the context and emergence of Celaya as an important villa between the mining regions of the north and Mexico City, see Solange Alberro, "Inquisición y proceso de cambio social: Delitos de hechicería en Celaya, 1614," *Revista de dialectología y tradiciones populares* 30, no. 3/4 (1974): 327–85.

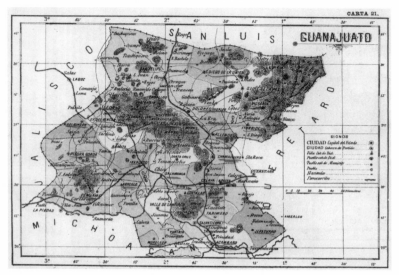

Fig. 5 Map of Guanajuato. From Antonio García Cubas, *Atlas metódico para la enseñanza de la geografía de la Republica Mexicana* (1899). Courtesy the David Rumsey Map Collection.

come forward and denounce any form of heresy, blasphemy, witch-craft, or any other crimes against the Church. In short order, in October and November, he heard denunciations and confessions from 115 individuals, most of whom claimed to have some knowledge of witchcraft or sorcery.[7] The documents that follow are representative samples.

A poor Spanish widow, Isabel Duarte, was the principal object of the accusations presented here. She, along with several other impov-erished women, was in many ways a typical social scapegoat who fell outside the normal protections of society. For example, the witnesses who denounced Duarte derisively called her *la junca* (the bulrush), a play on words from the family name of her deceased husband, Junco, and possibly a reference to a thin, malnourished body. Hers is a classic case of a widowed woman accused of witchcraft by meddling neighbors who may have had their own crimes to cover up. It is not entirely clear what exactly had transpired in Celaya and the sur-rounding areas. Various individuals came forth to make statements about what appear to be widespread practices of folk medicine. Some

7. Detailed in Alberro, ibid.

witnesses claimed that the women involved were witches, while others viewed these activities as forms of divination. Others said some women were part of a coven of witches who could fly.

Historian Solange Alberro has examined the perceived outbreak of witchcraft in Celaya as a prototypical manifestation of socioeconomic concerns that lead to accusations of witchcraft. Witchcraft was rarely prosecuted by Spanish Inquisitions, and in most cases such persecutions occurred in remote or mountain areas such as in the Basque country in Spain.[8] Such outbreaks were usually expressions of distrust of certain members of the community—widows, sexually active single women, outsiders, the mentally disturbed, or the very poor. Alberro offers a corollary interpretation. At the turn of the sixteenth century, the Spanish citizenry of Celaya had only recently begun to receive land grants, and an emerging group of Spaniards was making economic and social strides upwards. Celaya offers a typical case of "witches" as women and men who came from underprivileged sectors of society. Of the women accused of witchcraft in Celaya, all came from the less wealthy Spanish families or were ethnically mixed and were outsiders from Tlazazalca and San Miguel who had not been raised in Celaya. Likewise, in Celaya, as was often the case in Mexico, the types of sorcery mentioned were not what we might call black magic. Rather, they were forms of divination: using kernels of corn, copal incense, and cotton string to discover sexual inclinations; mixing menstrual blood in chocolate to "tame" husbands and lovers; and using herbs for abortion and to alleviate menstrual cramps. Other women claimed to have been able to fly after anointing themselves.

The Inquisition, in Spain and Mexico, was suspicious of the reality of witchcraft and tended to avoid prosecuting it except when inquisitors believed an express pact with the devil had taken place. For example, between 1625 and 1627, a decade after the Celaya case, 197 of the 365 denunciations that the inquisitors in Mexico received from their regional deputies concerned some form of witchcraft or spell-casting. And Alberro shows that between 1626 and 1630 in New Spain overall about 33 percent of all denunciations to the Inquisition involved charges of witchcraft, sorcery, or spell-casting. But in

8. For an excellent overview of this issue and of the Basque region prosecutions in particular as well, see Gustav Henningsen, *The Witches' Advocate: Basque Witchcraft and the Spanish Inquisition (1609–1614)* (Reno: University of Nevada Press, 1980).

that same period the Inquisition prosecuted only 5 of these cases of supposed witchcraft. In the first century of activity in Mexico (1527–1640), witchcraft represented only 5 percent of the cases that the Inquisition prosecuted.[9] The inquisitors' response to accusations of witchcraft was usually to ignore them; they simply did not believe that witchcraft was real and viewed it as a local issue.

Muñoz himself was quite skeptical about the reality of any pacts with the devil or sorcery in Celaya. The inquisitional familiar (deputized spy) Pedro Núñez de la Roxa appears to have taken advantage of social rivalries in the villa. The five women accused of sorcery were targets of social taunting—called "sluts," "retards," and "sorceresses" by the Spanish population of Celaya—and Núñez de la Roxa fanned the hysteria in an attempt to curry favor with the inquisitors in Mexico.[10]

The Celaya case gives us a rare glimpse at a written response of the Inquisition to its deputy. On February 19, 1615, the inquisitors issued vague and somewhat bland orders to Celaya for twenty-one women and five men to be reprimanded for their various activities in divination and sorcery.[11] The form of their punishment was not given, and it does not appear that for most of them it was to be very serious. In one case, Francisco Puntilla, an African *curandero* (healer), was convicted of being a "trickster." The inquisitors ordered that he be "gravely punished" with two hundred lashes, but only if he returned to his use of herbs in curing people. Blacks, *mestizos,* and foreigners (French and English) were more likely to be harshly punished than Spaniards by the Inquisition, and in all likelihood the other twenty-five accused were given mild scoldings in private settings. This was a common form of punishment by *comisarios* in local, remote settings, as in the diocese of Michoacán under Muñoz's care. Contrary to popular imagery, none of these individuals was ever burned at the stake.

The formulaic nature of the denunciations reproduced here is evident. Inquisitional interrogations were regulated by an extensive

9. See the data in Martin Austin Nesvig, "Pearls Before Swine: Theory and Practice of Censorship in New Spain, 1527–1640" (Ph.D. diss., Yale University, 2004), app. 3, and AGN, Inq., vol. 356, exp. 6 and vol. 360, exp. 1, cited in Nesvig, *Ideology and Inquisition,* 183–84.

10. See Alberro's discussion of the case ("Inquisición y proceso de cambio social").

11. AGN, Inq., vol. 305, exp. 11, cited and quoted in Alberro, "Inquisición y proceso de cambio social," 383–85.

body of both church and penal law. Church law regulated the inquisitional interview as a form of confession and established parameters for the nature of the oath and the scope of authority for the Inquisition. Penal law also established the way that interrogations could be made, and whether witnesses or suspects could be imprisoned. In general, there were two kinds of witnesses—those who appeared of their own volition and those who were summoned. Inquisitional testimonies in theory were secret, and breaking the secrecy of the chamber was itself a punishable offense, but it is obvious that secrecy of these statements made before Muñoz was not kept very well. This is not surprising given that Celaya was a small town.

Inquisitional documentation in Mexico tends to be one-directional. *Comisarios* like Muñoz conducted investigations, heard confessions and denunciations, took witness statements, and recorded this information in formal depositions. The documentation generated from this activity was then mailed to the inquisitors in Mexico City. The physical archives of the Mexican Inquisition remained extant through the colonial period, and as a result today we have access to a great deal of documentation sent from local *comisarios* to the Inquisition's offices in Mexico City. But we have very little of the documentation sent from the inquisitors to local *comisarios*—the letters, the instructions about legal procedure, the orders to arrest and send suspected heretics to Mexico City for trial.

Most local *comisarios* kept the correspondence sent to them from the inquisitors in Mexico City in their personal possession (if they kept it at all), rather than in a centralized archive or repository. After their deaths it passed to family members and over the centuries disappeared. Muñoz himself probably kept his correspondence in Acahuato, a remote outpost of the Franciscan mission in Michoacán, where after his death it may simply have been left to rot and deteriorate. It is all but certain that it does not exist today. For the *comisarios* who were attached to the local cathedral chapter or parish church, the documentation was, in theory, kept under lock and key. But as many cathedrals were decimated during various wars, revolutions, and state-sponsored expropriations of Church property in the nineteenth century, that material was frequently lost. Very little of this kind of documentation remains today, even in places with large cathedrals, like Valladolid.

The result is that the material sent by *comisarios* like Muñoz to the inquisitors represents some of the richest material left to us about local customs in early colonial rural Mexico. His depositions record in exacting detail a multitude of local customs—stews, spells, sexual habits, tattoos, crops, eating habits, family connections, religious festivals, preference for certain saints, the use and location of saint images, and much more.

Diego Muñoz
"Witness Statements in Celaya About Witchcraft" (1614)[12]

Interrogation of Pedro Hernández de Uribe
Concerning Leonor de Villareal, Isabel Rodríguez and Isabel de Aguiar

OATH

In the villa of Celaya, province and diocese of Michoacán of New Spain, on 17 October 1614, before Fray Diego Muñoz of the Order of Lord Saint Francis, and by his order and by virtue of the commission of the Holy Office, and before me, Fray Ambrosio Carrillo, notary, a Spanish man appeared (having been summoned), and swore in the form according to the law, to state the truth, who said he was called
Pedro Hernández de Uribe, married, originally of Apaseo in this diocese, and citizen of this villa, 37 or 38 years old, of sound mind and reason.
And he was asked
1st. If he knows of any person who has said or done anything that is or seems to be against the Holy Catholic Faith and Evangelic Law, which the Holy Mother Church of Rome holds, preaches and teaches.
He said that three months ago he went to a small Indian hamlet which is on the outskirts of this villa to buy some birds. On arriving at a house of an Indian he heard that some people inside were speaking Spanish. He stopped to listen to the conversation, and it sounded like women. One said to the other, "enough! They have summoned us before Pero Núñez, the familiar of the Holy Office,

12. AGN, Inq., vol. 278, exp. 2, fol. 183.

and he has summoned me." And the other said that she also had been summoned in order to take her statement, and that these women did not stop with this but they said that they were flyers [*voladoras*]. And, they seeming to him to be common people, he entered where they were and said to them, "Congratulations, flying women!" They responded quite confused that he knew the name, and he said to them that having heard it he greeted them with it. And they were Leonor de Villareal, *mestiza*, single, and Isabel Rodríguez [here the notary comments, "although he is wrong about the last name"], who is also the *mestiza* wife of Marcos Ramírez. With this he left.

And a month later, after going with Raphael Hernández, a citizen of this villa, to the same little hamlet of Indians, around nine in the evening, they saw a bulky figure which was going along the plains. And since it was dark and drizzling, they could not discern what it was. And this witness then recognized it and saw that it was the said Isabel, wife of Marcos Ramírez, who was wrapped in a cape and alone, and she became angry that they had recognized her. And Raphael Hernández reprimanded her because he thought it was improper that she was walking alone in the countryside at that hour. And this witness suspected that she was up to something evil.

His statement was read to him, and he said it was correctly written and represents what he knows as the truth, and he affirmed it and signed under oath. And he was warned that it must be ratified and he would be called again and that in the interim he should search his memory in case he needs to strike, add to, or amend his statement.

Secrecy. He was sworn to secrecy under pain of excommunication and promised to uphold it.

Fray Diego Muñoz

Pero Hernández de Uribe

Before me, Fray Ambrosio Carrillo, notary

Report to the Holy Office of the Inquisition of this New Spain [given by Fray Diego Muñoz] against Isabel Duarte, the bulrush, for sorcery[13]

The following persons testified:

---

13. AGN, Inq., vol. 278, exp. 4, fols. 176–209. The numeration varies and is occasionally inconsistent with the internal numeration, suggesting there are lost sections.

—Gerónimo de Vergara, Spaniard
—María Victoria, black
—María Madalena de la Cruz, Spaniard
—Francisca Gutiérrez, Spaniard
—Leonor de Hinojosa, Spaniard
—doña María de Velasco, Spaniard
—Felipa de Sanctiago, black
—Isabel Lucía, *ladina* Indian[14]
—Margarita López, Spaniard
—Francisco de Contreras, *mestizo*
—Joan Pantaleón, Tarascan Indian
—Fabián de Oviedo, Spaniard
—Francisca de Raya y Arenas, Spaniard
—María de Torres, Spaniard
—Isabel de Vallejo, Spaniard
—Isabel María, *mulata*
This woman is considered slightly retarded but not in such a way
(as far as I can discern and I am informed) that she lacks reason,
and it stands to reason, as far as I infer, that she does not sin from
ignorance. Years earlier (this is publicly known in the villa) she was
punished with a fine by the ordinary [a local ecclesiastical magistrate]
for sorcery. In the deposition made on the case of fortunetelling of
Fabián de Oviedo, she dissembles and excuses herself, blaming the
Indian Pantaleón, whom she offers as a scapegoat,[15] in order to attri-
bute the blame to him and to escape punishment, as it is known that
the Holy Office does not prosecute Indians. I questioned him [the

14. This usually meant an Indian who could speak Spanish, though it was also
used to denote an Indian more acculturated to Spanish dress and custom. In some cases
it also referred to an Indian who was *ladino* in some other indigenous language that
was not the language learned in childhood. For example, an Otomí Indian who spoke
Nahuatl might be referred to as an "indio ladino en lengua mexicana." But the most
common use was to denote an Indian who was linguistically or culturally hispanicized
to some extent.

15. The phrase used is "al qual debieron tomar los dos por cabeza de lobo." In the
seventeenth century the phrase meant to offer someone up as a distraction (i.e., a "red
herring"). The *Real Academia Española* defines it as "cosa que se exhibe u ostenta para
atraer o recompensar el favor de los demás." The term also can refer to a dupe, a sacri-
ficial goat, or a wolf in sheep's clothing. It was also used to mean to attract the favor of
others, as used in the 1528 *La lozana andaluza;* see Juan Pablo Torrente, *Osos y otras
fieras en el pasado de Asturias (1700–1860)* (Proaza: Fundación Oso de Asturias, 1999),
151. Also see Angel Flores, ed. and trans., *Spanish Stories: Cuentos Españoles: Stories*

Indian Pantaleón], and he testified that the bulrush had told fortunes. This is more likely given what was said about her and because it has not been noted that the Indian was a sorcerer, and being as he is of the Tarascan nation, they are not inclined to sorcery anyway. And Fray Sebastián Alemán, his guardian (whom he knows and treats as the ordinary), informs me that Pantaleón assists him and serves as cantor in the church and that he has not known him to have anything to do with sorcery.

I also questioned Fabián de Oviedo, and although he continues to deny any charges, this does not provide a valid excuse. He comes to confess the guilt of the fortunetelling and the intent to commit it on account of the woman with whom he was in a relationship. Because she had left him (this is publicly known in this villa), he had wanted to kill her, and he wounded her face, by which he marked her as a married woman. I saw this wound. She is considered extremely jealous of her husband, and Oviedo is considered reckless and insolent by all. The statements by him and the bulrush (which Pedro Núñez de la Roxa received) disagree in part with those declarations I received. This woman is a widow and considered impoverished.

And given the deposition of Leonor de Hinojosa, it appears that she [presumably Isabel Duarte] mixed holy words and blessings with superstitions and invocations of demons when she said to her that she spoke with three demons. And Doña María de Velasco declares that when she cast lots she said that three demons pursued her husband and persuaded him to try to kill her.

Fray Diego Muñoz

SORCERY

Margarita López, Spaniard, against Isabel Duarte, the bulrush
In the villa of Celaya, province and diocese of Michoacán of New Spain, on 3 November 1614, before Fray Diego Muñoz of the Order

---

in the Original Spanish with New English Translations (New York: Dover, 1987), 281: "una cabeza de lobo, a dupe." I wish to thank many people for their generosity with help on this term: Javier Villa-Flores, Rigoberto Rodríguez, Matthew O'Hara, Brian Owensby, Galen Brokaw, Javier Puente-Valdivia, Carlos D. Paz, David Rex-Galindo, Charles Beatty-Medina, Alex Hidalgo, Miguel Costa, Christopher Conway, and Tom Holloway—all of whom weighed in on what was a most fruitful H-Latam posting.

of Lord Saint Francis, *comisario* of the Holy Office of the Inquisition, and before me, Fray Ambrosio Carrillo, notary, a Spanish woman appeared (without having been summoned) and swore according to the law to state the truth, who said she is called

Margarita López, born in Mexico City, citizen of this villa of Celaya, wife of Domingo Ochoa de Ibarra, and forty years old.

1st. Asked the reason for having appeared before the said *comisario*, she responded that it is in fulfillment of the general edict of the faith and to unburden her conscience.

And thus verbally proposed the reason she comes to make a statement she was advised to make her statement in the form of a deposition and thus she understood.

She said and declared that one day in the afternoon twenty years ago she was in the house of Mari Ramos, citizen of this villa and now widow of Hernando de Manduxana, along with María Magdalena, the mother-in-law of Quintanilla and of Cachal Mencía Riquelme, when they saw Gerónimo de Vergara, tailor, employee of Diego de Junco (the husband of Isabel Duarte de la Cruz), drinking spoonfuls of cacao from a gourd. He pulled out of the chocolate some things like threads or fibers which were colored like dried chile, and María Magdalena, wife of Joan Freile, who was also present, warned him that it was blood. He continued to drink it, and she said, "God help me, it is blood!" He took notice of this and with a finger rubbed a fiber on the floor and saw that it was true. He was horrified, his stomach roiled, and he began to vomit. He said that his master, Diego de Junco, had drunk part of the cacao and that he had given it to him, and he complained to Isabel Duarte that she had given the cacao to her husband because she had tried to excuse herself from it by blaming an Indian woman who had ground the cacao. But the Indian woman admitted that she had brought the cacao in powder as ordered and the bulrush made the cacao in her house.

2nd. If she knows any person who has done anything that is or appears to be against the Holy Catholic Faith and Evangelic Law which the Holy Mother Church of Rome preaches and teaches.

She responded that she has heard some things about witches and sorceries that are not exactly certain and that she does not know anything in particular.

She was read her statement, and she said that it was correctly written and represents the truth. She affirmed this under oath and did not sign her name. She was warned that having been summoned she will have to ratify her statement and that in the interim she should search her memory in case she needs to strike from, add to, or amend her statement.

Secrecy. She was sworn to secrecy under pain of excommunication and promised to guard that secrecy.

Fray Diego Muñoz
Before me, Fray Ambrosio Carrillo, notary

[Casting] Lots

Interrogation of Fabián de Oviedo, Spaniard. He accuses and deposes against the bulrush.

In the villa of Celaya, province and diocese of Michoacán of New Spain, on 28 November 1614, before the father Fray Diego Muñoz of the Order of Lord Saint Francis, by the mandate in virtue of the commission of the Holy Office of the Inquisition and before me, Fray Ambrosio Carrillo, notary, a Spanish man appeared (having been summoned) and swore according to the law to state the truth, who said he was called

Fabián de Oviedo, originally of Mexico City, married, citizen of this villa of Celaya, and twenty-two years old.

1st. Asked if he knows or presumes the reason for having been summoned, he said that he presumes that it is because he made a declaration before Pedro Núñez de la Roxa, familiar of the Holy Office, seven months ago, and that he was ordered to mention this.

He stated and declared that in that same time one day after Mass he was next to the church of Saint Augustine in this villa and he came across a woman they call the bulrush (considered somewhat retarded and who is often mocked). She asked this witness why he was so thin and what did he have to keep himself so thin. And joking he responded to her that he was sick with love and asked her to give him something for it. And she offered to give him something that she would acquire from a comadre[16] of hers and that she would bring it to him at his house. In the evening she went to his house and brought him two little sticks like little darts and told him he should

16. A godmother to one's child but also a general term of fictional familial bond in which two women (or two men in the case of compadres) share a kind of mutual obligation and reciprocal kinship for each other and each others' families.

chew them. After chewing them he should rub his hands and face and then pass through the door of any woman he desired and remove his hat and then she would call him. And this witness considered this to be a fraud and threw away the sticks, not paying any attention to it.

Three days later he came across her in a street, and she asked him how it went. And he responded, "Go with God"—that those were tricks. And she said that he had not taken advantage of them and she would bring an Indian named Pantaleón and that he would have to show him the woman he wants and that she would let him know when the Indian was at home. Later, one day at two in the afternoon he sent to call on a young woman and went to the house of the Indian and found the Indian there. The three of them [presumably Juana Duarte was the third] went alone into a room. Closing the door and placing a jar of water on the floor, the Indian asked their names, saying it was necessary for what he was going to do. This witness told him his name and the name of the young woman with whom he had a relationship. Pantaleón threw two kernels of maize symbolic of their names into the jar, and the Indian threw one on his accord, saying that it went in the name of the husband of the young woman. He also threw another seven or eight kernels without names, and on some coals he threw what seemed to be some myrrh. Taking the jar in his hands and placing it over the smoke, it seemed to him that he moved his hands. With this movement the maize kernels moved, and two of them came together and a third remained apart.

The Indian interpreted—the bulrush asked him if the woman had betrayed this witness, which was, in the end, the purpose of doing all this—the two kernels as being those of the names of this witness, and the woman and that she had not betrayed him and that the third kernel which remained apart was that of the husband and that because of this he would die within three months. But this was a lie, as seven months have passed and the man is still alive. Later one of the two kernels separated, and the Indian said it was that in the name of the woman and that it separated only because she was not with any other man. And he threw the lots two times in the same way in two different days. And at that time this witness had a stomach illness, and the Indian cured him by sucking his navel and sprinkling it with water. And it seemed to him [the witness] that he spat out something which he took from his navel, and he said that the sickness was of a morsel and that with this cure he would be fine. And after this a few days later, recalling what the Indian and the bulrush had done, he thought that it was not good but rather it seemed to him to be a demonic art. So he went to clear his conscience by making a declaration before Pedro Núñez de la Roxa, the familiar of the Holy Office. And he accused himself and asked for mercy. And for the guilt he bears for this he returns now to accuse himself and ask for mercy with Christian, Catholic remorse. And when they threw the lots he did not consider it with attention and he accused himself.

2nd. If he knows anyone who has done or said anything that is or seems to be against the Holy Catholic Faith and Evangelic Law that the Holy Mother Church of Rome holds, preaches, and teaches.

He responded that he does not know more than what he declared.

He was read his statement, and under oath he said it was correctly written and the truth of what he knows [and he signed below]. And he was warned that today six hours later he would have to ratify his statement and that he should search his memory in case he needs to strike from, add to, or amend his statement.

Secrecy. He was sworn to secrecy under pain of excommunication, and he swore to keep it.

Fabián de Oviedo
Fray Diego Muñoz
Before me, Fray Ambrosio Carrillo, notary

SPELLS

Isabel Duarte de la Cruz, concerning Fabián de Oviedo

In the villa of Celaya, province and diocese of Michoacán in New Spain on 27 November 1614 before Fray Diego Muñoz of the Order of Lord Saint Francis, *comisario* of the Holy Office of the Inquisition, and before me, Fray Ambrosio Carrillo, notary, a Spanish woman appeared (having been summoned) and swore according to the law, who said she is called

Isabel Duarte de la Cruz, originally of the villa of San Miguel in this diocese of Michoacán, citizen of this villa of Celaya, widow of Diego de Junco, and fifty years old.

Asked if she knows or presumes the reason she has been summoned, she responded no.

If she remembers having made any declaration before a minister of the Holy Office and on what matter, she responded that about four months ago she make a declaration in this villa concerning Fabián de Oviedo, Spaniard, before Pedro Núñez de la Roxa, familiar of the Holy Office, and that he ordered her to report here.

She said and declared that about five months ago she was returning home after hearing Mass in Saint Augustine in this villa when Fabián de Oviedo, a merchant citizen of this villa, came across her. He put his hands on her and begged and pleaded with her with great passion to give him something so that a niece of this witness would love him because she had left him. And she responded to him, "I am a horse that does not know anything of such things." He continued to beg her for this another five times on different days, and finally she grew tired. Irritated, she told him to look for an Indian named Pantaleón because they say he knows things and that he is known for finding things that have been stolen or lost. And eight days later around noon she was alone at home when she saw the Indian come in through a door, and through another door came Fabián de Oviedo (the house has two doors), and he must have brought the Indian because this witness did not call him. And the Indian asked for a jar of water and some kernels of maize, and she brought them to him because at that time there was no one else in her house. And the three of them present, the Indian threw a large handful into the jar and also put some *copal* [aromatic resin used as incense] on some coals for which he had asked and she had brought to him. And he put the jar so close to the coals that it was bathed in smoke, and as he shook the jar a little with his hands the kernels began to move until the smoke began to subside. And the Indian told Fabián de Oviedo not to worry, that he should go to where the woman lived and that she would be at the door and call for him and she would no longer be angry.

She was read her statement, and she said that it was correctly written and represents the truth, repeating the oath she swore earlier, and she did not sign her name. And she was warned that having been summoned she would be asked to ratify her statement and that in the interim she should search her memory in case she needs to strike from, add to, or amend her statement.

Secrecy. She was sworn to secrecy under pain of excommunication, and she promised to uphold it.

Fray Diego Muñoz
Before me, Fray Ambrosio Carrillo, notary

Spells

María Victoria, black, against Isabel Duarte

In the villa of Celaya, province and diocese of Michoacán in New Spain, on 21 October 1614 before Fray Diego Muñoz of the Order of Lord Saint Francis, *comisario* of the Holy Office of the Inquisition, and before me, Fray Ambrosio Carrillo, notary, a Guinean black woman, more *ladina* than *bozal*,[17] appeared (not having been summoned) and swore according to the law, who said she is called

María Victoria, originally from Cazanga, slave of Isabel Gutiérrez, forty years old, and is she previously mentioned by Felipa de Sanctiago, black.

1st. Asked the reason for having appeared before the said *comisario*, she said that in order to unburden her conscience she declares the following

That a year ago Isabel Duarte the bulrush asked her if her mistress abused her and she offered her something with which to tame her so that that she could come and go from the house as she pleased. She asked her for money for this, and she responded that she did not need it because her mistress treated her well and let her leave the house when she did not have anything to do.

2nd. If she knows anyone who has done or said anything that is or seems to be against the Holy Catholic Faith and Evangelic Law which the Holy Church of Rome holds, preaches, and teaches.

She said that she only had heard gossip that the said Isabel Duarte and Mari Vázquez, black, are sorceresses, and she does not know anything particular more than what she has declared. Also Melchiora, black, of Bernabé Hernández, discovered a few days ago that Felipa, black, her *compañera*, was looking for something with which to tame her owner.

She was read her statement and said that it was correctly written, under the same oath she swore, and did not sign her name.

And she was warned that having been called she would have to ratify her statement and that in the interim she should search her memory in case she needs to strike from, add to or amend it.

17. As with Indians, black Africans who were linguistically or culturally Hispanicized were referred to as *ladinos*. *Bozal* was a term for a black African who was not at all hispanicized and usually meant someone who did not understand Spanish.

Secrecy. She was sworn to secrecy under pain of excommunication and she promised to uphold it.

Fray Diego Muñoz
Before me, Fray Ambrosio Carrillo, notary

Spells

María Magdalena de la Cruz, Spaniard, against Isabel Duarte
In the villa of Celaya, province and diocese of Michoacán in New Spain, on 23 November 1614 before Fray Diego Muñoz of the Order of Lord Saint Francis, *comisario* of the Holy Office of the Inquisition, and before me, Fray Ambrosio Carrillo, notary, a Spanish woman appeared (without being summoned) and swore according to the law who said she is called

María Magdalena de la Cruz, originally from the villa of San Miguel of this diocese of Michoacán, wife of Joan de Vargas, he a citizen of this villa of Celaya, and fifty-six years old.

1st. Asked the reason for having appeared before the said *comisario*, she responded that it is in fulfillment of and obedience to the general edict of the faith and to unburden her conscience.

And thus verbally proposed the reason she comes to make a statement she was advised to make her statement in the form of a deposition and thus she understood.

She said and declared that about four years ago it became widely known in this villa that Isabel Duarte de la Cruz was a sorceress. This witness (being her sister) warned her of this, and reprimanding her for this she advised her that she should go to Mexico City to accuse herself, but she refused to do so.

And about three months ago another case of casting lots in a jar of water in which her sister was being accused became widely known. She again advised her that she go to accuse herself before the Holy Office, and she responded that she had been pestered to bring the Indian, who cast the lots, to her house, and that she would go to accuse herself.

And Leonor de Hinojosa, daughter of this witness, told her that the said Isabel Duarte had cast lots in her house and that she found it very wicked, and this refers to what her daughter stated.

And it could have been about four or five years ago that a young virgin [*doncella*] Inés, daughter of Joan Sánchez Badillo and Francisca

Zamora, died in this villa, and it was well known and a common opinion that she had died from a spell cast by the black woman Mari Vázquez with a large fingernail that she had placed in her hand. And this refers to what Francisca Zamora, mother of the deceased, said and which this witness heard.

2nd. If she knows anyone who has said or done anything that is or appears to be against the Holy Catholic Faith and Evangelic Law that the Holy Mother Church of Rome holds, preaches, and teaches. She said no.

She was read her statement, and she said it was correctly written and represents the truth under the oath which she affirmed, and she did not sign her name. And she was warned that she will have to ratify her statement and that in the interim she should search her memory in case she needs to strike from, add to, or amend it.

Secrecy. She was sworn to secrecy under pain of excommunication and promised to uphold it.

Fray Diego Muñoz
Before me, Fray Ambrosio Carrillo, notary

SPELLS

In the villa of Celaya, province and diocese of Michoacán in New Spain, on 27 October 1614 before Fray Diego Muñoz of the Order of Lord Saint Francis, *comisario* of the Holy Office of the Inquisition, and before me, Fray Ambrosio Carrillo, notary, a black *ladina* woman appeared (without being summoned) and swore according to the law who said she is called

Felipa de Sanctiago, originally of the City of Angels [Puebla], slave of Bernabé de Hernández, ensign [*alférez*] of the villa of Celaya, married and thirty years old.

1st. Asked the reason for having appeared before the said *comisario*, she responded that it was in fulfillment of and obedience to the general edict of the faith and to unburden her conscience.

And thus verbally proposed the reason she comes to make a statement, she was advised to make her statement in the form of a deposition and thus she understood.

She said that six months ago she was talking with Isabel Duarte the bulrush in her house and saw that the black woman Catalina asked her for something to tame her mistress. And she took a raw egg and cracked it open and threw inside it some little balls of cotton, taking them into her mouth; she could not understand what she said. And she gave it to the said Catalina, saying, take it and bury it and you will see how well things go with your mistress. And this witness asked Isabel Duarte, "Ma'am, what are you doing there?" and she responded, "If you knew what I was doing you would be terrified."

And a year ago a silver knife belonging to her mistress went missing, and she went to Isabel Duarte to ask her to make it appear because it was said that she knows so much. And Duarte took a large jar full of clear water and she placed it on the floor and she threw into it kernels of maize, each of which was wrapped in cotton. And then she asked for a stub of a lit candle and a head rag of this witness. She passed the candle in front of the jar three times from one hand to the other and then put it in the middle of the jar and moved the candle with the rag. Later she put out the candle, attesting that the knife would appear, but it did not appear. And as payment she asked for a hen, and she gave it to her.

The general edict of the faith having been read, the said Isabel Duarte went to the house of this witness, and another time she called on her, and every time she begged her not to say what she knew before the *comisario* of the Holy Office. And obeying her (she had begged her earnestly), she told her she would not say anything. And the truth is that she had made a statement. And she also begged her to speak with Victoria Selaba of Isabel Gutiérrez so that she say nothing and that she chided María, the black woman of the widow of Joan de Quintanilla, who said she was a witch and sorceress. And she did not tell them anything. And it is publicly said in this town that the said Isabel Duarte is a sorceress.

2nd. If she knows anyone who has said or done anything that is or appears to be against the Holy Catholic Faith and Evangelic Law that the Holy Mother Church of Rome holds, preaches, and teaches.

She said no.

She was read her statement, and she said it was correctly written and represents the truth under the oath which she affirmed, and she did not sign her name. And she was warned that she will have to ratify her statement and that in the interim she should search her memory in case she needs to strike from, add to, or amend it.

Secrecy. She was sworn to secrecy under pain of excommunication and promised to uphold it.

Fray Diego Muñoz

Before me, Fray Ambrosio Carrillo, notary

SPELLS

Gerónimo de Vergara, Spaniard, against Isabel Duarte, the bulrush

In the villa of Celaya, province and diocese of Michoacán in New Spain, on 20 October 1614 before Fray Diego Muñoz of the Order of Lord Saint Francis, *comisario* of the Holy Office of the Inquisition, and before me, Fray Ambrosio Carrillo, notary, a Spanish man appeared (without being summoned) and swore according to the law who said he is called

Gerónimo de Vergara, originally from Seville, citizen of this villa of Celaya, married, and forty-five years old.

1st. Asked the reason for having appeared before the said *comisario*, he responded that it is in fulfillment of and obedience to the general edict of the faith and to unburden his conscience.

And thus verbally proposed the reason he comes to make a statement he was advised to make his statement in the form of a deposition and thus he understood.

He said and declared that about twenty years ago when he was single he was speaking with some women in the house of Isabel Duarte the bulrush, who gave him some gourds of cacao or chocolate. And this witness took one and drank some spoonfuls from it, and he pulled out of it some things that looked like fibers of chiles that were not well ground. And María Magdalena, mother-in-law of Joan de Quintanilla, warned him that it was not chile but rather menstrual blood. And he threw a long, thin clot on the floor and saw that it was blood, and he began to feel rather ill as he came to realize that it had come from the cacao which he drank. And he went to tell Isabel Duarte how this had happened. And she responded that it was not for him but for her husband in order to tame him, and she closed the jar.

Twenty-six or twenty-seven years ago, when Diego de Junco, the husband of Isabel Duarte, was still alive, he ate the midafternoon meal with them in their house. After the meal the husband and wife retired for a siesta and this witness remained in the sitting room [*sala*]. After a while he left, screaming out and complaining grievously of his natural part [groin], which was inflamed, in which this witness saw what looked like ground *pepitas* [squash seeds] but which he could not identify. And with cold water and lard he was able to cool it down. And he told his wife about this and how he did not know what that evil woman had given him. And she asked him what it was and he became angry and slapped her.

2nd. If he knows anyone who has said or done anything that is or appears to be against the Holy Catholic Faith and Evangelic Law that the Holy Mother Church of Rome holds, preaches and teaches.

He said that it was rumored that there are witches in this villa, but he does not know anything particular.

He was read his statement, and he said it was correctly written and the truth under the oath which he affirmed, and he knows how to sign his name.

He was warned that he will have to ratify his statement and that in the interim he should search his memory in case he needs to strike from, add to, or amend it.

Secrecy. He was sworn to secrecy under pain of excommunication and promised to uphold it.

Gerónimo de Vergara
Fray Diego Muñoz
Before me, Fray Ambrosio Carrillo, notary

SPELLS

Francisca Gutiérrez, Spaniard, against Isabel Duarte, the bulrush

In the villa of Celaya, province and diocese of Michoacán in New Spain, on 22 October 1614 before Fray Diego Muñoz of the Order of Lord Saint Francis, *comisario* of the Holy Office of the Inquisition, and before me, Fray Ambrosio Carrillo, notary, a Spanish woman appeared (without being summoned) and swore according to the law who said she is called

Francisca Gutiérrez, a virgin and originally from this villa of Celaya, daughter of Joan de Vargas and María Magdalena, 25 years old.

1st. Asked the reason for having appeared before the said *comisario*, she responded that it is in fulfillment of and obedience to the general edict of the faith and to unburden her conscience.

And thus verbally proposed the reason she comes to make a statement she was advised to make her statement in the form of a deposition, and thus she understood.

She said and declared that a year and a half ago Leonor de Hinojosa, her sister, told her that in this villa in her presence Isabel Duarte de la Cruz, their aunt, had cast lots with a jug of water and maize kernels, invoking three demons to see if the husband of Leonor de Hinojosa had a concubine because he was giving her an evil life, and this refers to what Leonor testified.

That about ten years ago, the villa receiving notice of the impending arrival of a prelate to this villa, Diego de Junco, husband of Isabel Duarte, spoke with María Magdalena de la Cruz, the mother of this witness, so that the case of some bones of dead people of which she was extremely protective not become known. And she [María Magdalena] went to the convent of Carmen to protect herself from the intervention of the friars.

And about seven years ago the said María Magdalena, her mother, told her that Fray Sebastián de Tamayo of the Order of Lord Saint Francis had advised her that she reprimand Isabel Duarte for giving the herb *doradilla*[18] to the Indian women so that their husbands would not abuse them.

And it could be about three years ago that a nephew of hers named Juan Gutiérrez told her that he was eating a quince with another boy, the son of Joan de Quintanilla, when a son of Joanna de Rodríguez (she does not know his name) had told them, "Give me that quince and I will give you something with which to combine it like my sisters smear on their waist and they attach a rag and can fly."

And recently about a month ago Agustín Muñiz, her brother-in-law, told her that on a bet between him and Joan de Cuenca, a citizen of this villa, he had come at night to the cemetery of Lord Saint Francis and had taken the dirt from the top of a grave and that he was accompanied by Isabel de Retamesa, aunt of Cuenca. And taking the dirt he gave it to her for a woman who wanted it in order to put it on her mother's pillow so that she could be invisible.

2nd. If she knows anyone who has said or done anything that is or appears to be against the Holy Catholic Faith and Evangelic Law that the Holy Mother Church of Rome holds, preaches, and teaches.

She said no.

18. *Doradilla* (*Ceterach officinarum*) is a small fern that grows out of fissures in rocks. It is known in Nahuatl as *yamanquitexochitl* and in Spanish as *flor de piedra* (flower of the rock). When prepared as a tea it acts as a diuretic and is used to alleviate kidney stones and to ease the release of the placenta.

She was read her statement, and she said it was correctly written and represents the truth of what she knows under the oath which she affirmed, and she signed her name. And she was warned that she will have to ratify her statement and that in the interim she should search her memory in case she needs to strike from, add to, or amend it.

Secrecy. She was sworn to secrecy under pain of excommunication and promised to uphold it.

Francisca Gutierres de Inojosa
Fray Diego Muñoz
Before me, Fray Ambrosio Carrillo, notary

BIBLIOGRAPHY

Abbreviations

AGI: Archivo General de las Indias, Seville, Spain.
AGN: Archivo General de la Nación, Mexico City, Mexico.
PG: Migne, Jacques-Paul. *Patrologiae cursus completus, Series Graeca.* Paris: Migne, 1857–66.
PL: Migne, Jacques-Paul. *Patrologiae cursus completus, Series Latina.* Paris: Migne, 1844–64.

Published Sources

"Actas originales de las congregaciones celebradas en 1527 para examinar las doctrinas de Erasmo." Análisis y extractos de Antonio Paz y Meliá y Manuel Serrano y Sanz. *Revista de Archivos, Bibliotecas y Museos* 6 (1902).
Aguirre Beltrán, Gonzalo. *Problemas de la población indígena de la Cuenca del Tepacaltepec.* Memorias del Instituto Nacional Indigenista, vol. 3. Mexico City: Ediciones del Instituto Nacional Indigenista, 1952.
Albaret, Laurent, ed. *Les Inquisiteurs: Portraits de défenseurs de la foi en Languedoc (XIIIe–XIVe siècles).* Toulouse: Editions Privat, 2001.
Alberro, Solange. "Inquisición y proceso de cambio social: Delitos de hechicería en Celaya, 1614." *Revista de dialectología y tradiciones populares* 30 (1974).
Alcalá, Jerónimo de. *La relación de Michoacán.* Morelia: Ayuntamiento de Morelia; Madrid: Testimonio Compañía Editorial, Patrimonio Nacional, 2001.
Almandoz Garmendía, José Antonio, ed. *Fray Alonso de Veracruz O.S.A. y la encomienda indiana en la historia eclesiástica novohispana (1522–1556): Edición crítica del texto* De dominio infidelium et iusto bello. Prologue by Ernest J. Burrus. Madrid: Porrúa Turanzas, 1971–77.
Anaissi, Tobia. *Bullarium Maronitarum.* Rome: n.p., 1922.

Angelomus of Luxeuil. *Ennarationes in libros Regum*. Rome: Apud Paulum Manutium, 1565.

Arévalo, Francisco de. *Sermón . . . día del Angélico Doctor Sancto Thomás de Aquino siete de março 1632*. Mexico City: n.p., 1632.

Astell, Ann W. "Cassiodorus's Commentary on the Psalms as an Ars rhetorica." *Rhetorica* 17 (1999).

Augustine. *De catechizandis rudibus*. PL, vol. 40.

———. *De doctrina christiana*. PL, vol. 34.

Bataillon, Marcel. *Erasmo y España: Estudios sobre la historia espiritual del siglo XVI*. Translated by Antonio Alatorre. Mexico City: Fondo de Cultura Económica, 1966.

Baudot, George. *Utopia and History: The First Chroniclers of Mexican Civilization (1520–1569)*. Translated by Bernard R. Ortiz de Montellano and Thelma Ortiz de Montellano. Niwot: University of Colorado Press, 1995.

Beaumont, Pablo de la Purísima Concepción. *Crónica de Michoacán*. Mexico City: Talleres Gráficos de la Nación, 1932.

Belda Plans, Juan. *La escuela de Salamanca y la renovación de la teología en el siglo XVI*. 2 vols. Madrid: Biblioteca de Autores Cristianos, 2000.

Bonaventure. "Las cinco festividades del niño Jesús." In *Obras de San Buenaventura*, vol. 2, ed. Fr. León Amorós, Bernardo Apperibay, and Miguel Oromi, 359–89. Madrid: Biblioteca de Autores Cristianos, 1957.

Brading, D. A. *The First America: The Spanish Monarchy, Creole Patriots, and the Liberal State, 1492–1867*. Cambridge: Cambridge University Press, 1991.

Burkhart, Louise M. *Holy Wednesday: A Nahua Drama from Early Colonial Mexico*. Philadelphia: University of Pennsylvania Press, 1996.

Bustos, Tomás de. *Santo Domingo de Guzmán: Predicador del Evangelio*. Salamanca: Editorial San Esteban, 2000.

Canedo, Lino G. *Educación de los marginados durante la época colonial: Escuelas y colegios para indios y mestizos en la Nueva España*. Mexico City: Porrúa, 1982.

Carreño, Alberto María. *Fr. Domingo de Betanzos: Fundador en la Nueva España de la venerable orden dominica*. Mexico City: Imprenta Victoria, 1924.

Carro, Venancio D. *La teología y los teólogos-juristas españoles ante la conquista de América*. 2 vols. Madrid: Talleres Gráficos Marsiego, 1944.

Cassiodorus, Flavius Magnus Aurelius. *Expositio in Cantica Canticorum*. PL, vol. 70.

Castillo, Santiago. *Alfonso de Castro y el problema de las leyes penales: O la obligatoriedad moral de las leyes humanas*. Salamanca: Universidad de Salamanca, 1941.

Castro, Alfonso de. *Adversus omnes haereses*. Cologne: ex officina Melchioris Novesiani, 1549.

———. *De justa haereticorum punitione*. Madrid: Ex typographia Blasii Roman, 1773.

Castro, Manuel de. "Fr. Alfonso de Castro, O.F.M. (1495–1558), consejero de Carlos V y Felipe II." *Salmanticensis* 6 (1958).

Chrysostom. *Homilia* 32. PG, vol. 57.

Chuchiak, John F., IV. "*In Servitio Dei:* Fray Diego de Landa, the Franciscan Order, and the Return of the Extirpation of Idolatry in the Colonial Diocese of Yucatán, 1573–1579." *Americas* 61 (2005).

———. "The Sins of the Fathers: Franciscan Missionaries, Parish Priests and the Sexual Conquest of the Yucatec Maya, 1545–1785." *Ethnohistory* 54 (2007).

Clendinnen, Inga. *Ambivalent Conquests: Maya and Spaniard in Yucatan, 1517–1570.* Cambridge: Cambridge University Press, 1987.

Cline, Sarah. "The Spiritual Conquest Reexamined: Baptism and Christian Marriage in Early Sixteenth-Century Mexico." In *The Church in Colonial Latin America,* ed. John W. Schwaller. Jaguar Books on Latin America 21. Wilmington, Del.: Scholarly Resources, 2000.

Dondaine, Antoine. "Le manuel de l'inquisiteur (1230–1330)." *Archivum Fratrum Praedicatorum* 18 (1947).

Ennis, Arthur. *Fray Alonso de la Vera Cruz, O.S.A. (1507–1584): A Study of His Life and His Contributions to the Religious and Intellectual Affairs of Early Mexico.* Louvain: E. Warny, 1957.

Escobar, Matías de. *Americana Thebaida.* Mexico City: Imprenta Victoria, 1924.

Espinosa, Isidro Félix de. *Crónica de la provincia franciscana de los apóstoles San Pedro y San Pablo de Michoacán.* Mexico City: Editorial Santiago, 1945.

Eusebius. *Historiae eclesiasticae.* PG, vol. 20.

Fernández Álvarez, Manuel, ed. *La Universidad de Salamanca.* Vol. 2, *Atmósfera intelectual y perspectivas de investigación.* Salamanca: Universidad de Salamanca, 1990.

Flores, Angel, ed. and trans. *Spanish Stories: Cuentos Españoles: Stories in the Original Spanish with New English Translations.* New York: Dover, 1987.

Gallegos Rocafull, José Manuel. *El pensamiento mexicano en los siglos XVI y XVII.* Mexico City: Centro de Estudios Filosóficos, 1951.

García Icazbalceta, Joaquín. "La destrucción de antigüedades." In *Opúsculos varios* 2, vol. 2 of *Obras.* Mexico City: Imprenta de V. Agüeros, 1896.

———. *Don Fray Juan de Zumárraga, primer obispo y arzobispo de México.* Mexico City: Porrúa, 1947.

Given, James B. *Inquisition and Medieval Society: Power, Discipline, and Resistance in Languedoc.* Ithaca: Cornell University Press, 1997.

Gorman, Michael. "The Commentary on Genesis of Angelomus of Luxeuil and Biblical Studies Under Lothar." *Studi medievali* 40 (1999).

Greenleaf, Richard. *Zumárraga and the Mexican Inquisition, 1536–1543.* Washington, D.C.: Academy of American Franciscan History, 1961.

Henningsen, Gustav. *The Witches' Advocate: Basque Witchcraft and the Spanish Inquisition (1609–1614).* Reno: University of Nevada Press, 1980.

Herveus Burgidolensis. *Commentaria in epistolas Pauli, in epist. I ad Cor.* PL, vol. 181.

Homza, Lu Ann. "Erasmus as Hero, or Heretic? Spanish Humanism and the Valladolid Assembly of 1527." *Renaissance Quarterly* 50 (1997).

Jerome. *Commentaria in Evangelium Mathei.* PL, vol. 26.

———. *De viris illustribus.* PL, vol. 23

Kobayashi, José María. *La educación como conquista (empresa franciscana en México).* Mexico City: El Colegio de México, 1974.

Ladurie, Emmanuel LeRoy. *Montaillou: The Promised Land of Error.* Translated by Barbara Bray. New York: Vintage, 1978.

Lara, Jaime. *City, Temple, Stage: Eschatological Architecture and Liturgical Theatrics in New Spain.* Notre Dame: University of Notre Dame Press, 2004.

Leclercq, Jean. *Jean de Paris el l'ecclésiologie du XIIIe siècle.* Paris: J. Vrin, 1942.

León-Portilla, Miguel. *Bernardino de Sahagún: Pionero de la antropología.* Mexico City: UNAM, 1999.

Livy. *Ab urbe condita libri.*

Lundberg, Magnus. "El clero indígena en Hispanoamérica: De la legislación a la implementación y práctica eclesiástica." *Estudios de historia novohispana* 38 (2008).

———. "Unity and Conflict: The Church Politics of Alonso de Montúfar, O.P., Archbishop of Mexico, 1554–1572." Ph.D. diss., Lund University, 2004.

Maguire, William Edward. *John of Torquemada, O.P.: The Antiquity of the Church.* Washington, D.C.: Catholic University of America Press, 1957.

Martínez Baracs, Rodrigo. *Caminos cruzados: Fray Maturino Gilberti en Perivan.* Zamora: Colegio de Michoacán; Mexico City: INAH, 2005.

Martínez Ferrer, Luis. *La penitencia en la primera evangelización de México (1523–1585).* Mexico City: Universidad Pontificia de México, 1998.

Márquez Joaquín, Pedro, ed. *¿Tarascos o Purépecha? Voces sobre antiguas y nuevas discusiones en torno al gentilicio michoacano.* Morelia: Universidad Michoacana de San Nicolás de Hidalgo, 2007.

Mathes, Michael. *Santa Cruz de Tlatelolco: La primera biblioteca académica de las Américas.* Mexico City: Secretaría de Relaciones Exteriores, 1982.

Miranda, José. *El erasmista mexicano: Fray Alonso Cabello.* Mexico City: UNAM, 1958.

Morales, Francisco. *Ethnic and Social Background of the Franciscan Friars in Seventeenth Century Mexico.* Washington, D.C.: Academy of American Franciscan History, 1973.

Muldoon, James. *Canon Law, the Expansion of Europe, and World Order.* Aldershot: Ashgate, 1998.

Mundy, John Hine, and Kennerly M. Woody, eds. *The Council of Constance: The Unification of the Church.* New York: Columbia University Press, 1961.

Muñoz, Diego. *Descripción de la provincia de San Pedro y San Pablo de Michoacán, en las Indias de la Nueva España*. Introduction by José Ramírez Flores. Guadalajara: Instituto Jalisciense de Antropología e Historia, 1965.

Nesvig, Martin Austin. *Ideology and Inquisition: The World of the Censors in Early Mexico*. New Haven: Yale University Press, 2009.

―――. "Pearls Before Swine: Theory and Practice of Censorship in New Spain, 1527–1640." Ph.D. diss., Yale University, 2004.

―――. "El sermón de un erasmista olvidado." *Boletín del Archivo General de la Nación* [México] 6, no. 5 (2004).

O'Donnell, James J. *Cassiodorus*. Berkeley: University of California Press, 1979.

O'Gorman, Edmundo. *Idea del descubrimiento de América: Historia de esa interpretación y crítica de sus fundamentos*. Mexico City: Centro de Estudios Filosóficos, 1951.

Olaechea Labayen, Juan B. "Opinión de los teólogos españoles sobre dar estudios mayores a los Indios." *Anuario de estudios americanos* 15 (1958).

Olarte, Teodoro. "Alfonso de Castro (1495–1558): Su vida, su tiempo y sus ideas filosóficas-jurídicas." Tesis de licenciatura, Universidad Nacional de Costa Rica, 1946.

Osorio Romero, Ignacio. *La enseñanza del latín a los indios*. Mexico City: UNAM, 1990.

Pagden, Anthony. *The Fall of Natural Man: The American Indian and the Origins of Comparative Ethnology*. Cambridge: Cambridge University Press, 1982.

Pardo, Osvaldo F. *The Origins of Mexican Catholicism: Nahua Rituals and Christian Sacraments in Sixteenth-Century Mexico*. Ann Arbor: University of Michigan Press, 2004.

Pennington, Kenneth. *Pope and Bishops: The Papal Monarchy in the Twelfth and Thirteenth Centuries*. Philadelphia: University of Pennsylvania Press, 1984.

Phelan, John Leddy. *The Millennial Kingdom of the Franciscans in the New World*. 2nd ed., revised. Berkeley: University of California Press, 1970.

Proceso inquisitorial del cacique de Tetzcoco, don Carlos Ometochtzin (Chichimecatecotl). Mexico City: Biblioteca Enciclopédica del Estado de México, 1980.

Pseudo-Jerome. *Quaestiones on the Book of Samuel*. Edited and translated by Avrom Saltman. Leiden: Brill, 1975.

Rabanus Maurus. *Expositio in Proverbia Salomensis*. PL, vol. 111.

Ramos, Demetrio, et al. *La ética en la conquista de América: Francisco de Vitoria y la escuela de Salamanca*. Madrid: Consejo Superior de Investigaciones Científicas, 1984.

Rea, Alonso de la. *Chrónica de la Órden de N. Seráphico P.S. Francisco, Provincia de S. Pedro y S. Pablo de Mechoacán en la Nueva España*. Mexico City: La viuda de Bernardo Calderón [Paula de Benavides], 1643.

Relaciones geográficas de la Diócesis de Michoacán, 1579–1580. Guadalajara: n.p., 1958.

Ricard, Robert. *The Spiritual Conquest of Mexico.* Translated by Lesley Byrd Simpson. Berkeley: University of California Press, 1982.

Rodríguez Molinero, Marcelino. *Origen español de la ciencia del derecho penal: Alfonso de Castro y su sistema penal.* Madrid: Cisneros, 1959.

Sahagún, Bernardino. *General History of the Things of New Spain.* 13 vols. Translated by Arthur J. O. Anderson and Charles E. Dibble. Santa Fe: School of American Research, 1950–1982.

———. *Psalmodia cristiana.* Translated by Arthur J. O. Anderson. Salt Lake City: University of Utah Press, 1993.

Saranyana, Josep Ignasi. "La eucaristía en la teología sacramentaria Americana del siglo XVI." In *Eucaristía y nueva evangelización: Actas del IV Simposio la Iglesia en España y América: Siglos XVI–XX.* Córdoba: CajaSur Obra Social y Cultural, 1994.

Simancas, Diego de. "La vida y cosas notables del señor Obispo de Zamora don Diego de Simancas . . ." In *Autobiografías y memorias,* ed. M. Serrano y Sanz. Madrid: Bailly, Bailliére é hijos, 1905.

Suleiman Salibi, Kamal. *A House of Many Mansions: The History of Lebanon Reconsidered.* London: I. B. Tauris, 1988.

Tellechea Idígoras, José Ignacio. *El arzobispo Carranza "Tiempos recios."* 4 vols. Salamanca: Publicaciones Universidad Pontificia; Fundación Universitaria Española, 2003–2007.

———. *El arzobispo Carranza y su tiempo.* 2 vols. Madrid: Ediciones Guardarrama, 1968.

Theophylactus. *Expositio in epistulam II ad Timoth.* PG, vol. 125.

Torrente, Juan Pablo. *Osos y otras fieras en el pasado de Asturias (1700–1860).* Proaza: Fundación Oso de Asturias, 1999.

Vitoria, Francisco de. *Political Writings.* Edited by Anthony Pagden and Jeremy Lawrance. Cambridge: Cambridge University Press, 1991.

Zaballa Beascoechea, Ana de, and Josep Ignasi Sarayana. "Bartolomé de Ledesma y su doctrina sobre los justos títulos." In *Actas del III Congreso Internacional sobre los Dominicos y el nuevo mundo.* Madrid: Editorial Deimos, 1991.

Zavala, Silvio. *Filosofía política en la conquista de América.* Mexico City: Fondo de Cultura Económica, 1947.

Zawart, Anscar. *The History of Franciscan Preaching and of Franciscan Preachers (1209–1927): A Bio-bibliographical Study.* New York: J. F. Wagner, 1928.

latin american originals

Series Editor | Matthew Restall

This series features primary source texts on colonial and nineteenth-century Latin America, translated into English, in slim, accessible, affordable editions that also make scholarly contributions. Most of these sources are being published in English for the first time, and represent an alternative to the traditional texts on early Latin America. The initial focus is on the conquest period in sixteenth-century Spanish America, but subsequent volumes include Brazil, as well as later centuries. The series features archival documents and printed sources originally in Spanish, Portuguese, Latin, and various Native American languages. The contributing authors are historians, anthropologists, art historians, and scholars of literature.

Matthew Restall is Edwin Erle Sparks Professor of Latin American History and Anthropology, and Director of Latin American Studies, at the Pennsylvania State University. He is co-editor of *Ethnohistory* journal. J. Michael Francis is Professor of Latin American History at the University of North Florida.

Associate Series Editor | J. Michael Francis

Board of Editorial Consultants
Noble David Cook | Edward F. Fischer | Susan Kellogg
Elizabeth W. Kiddy | Kris E. Lane | Alida C. Metcalf
Susan Schroeder | John F. Schwaller | Ben Vinson III

Titles in print
Invading Colombia: Spanish Accounts of the
Gonzalo Jiménez de Quesada Expedition of Conquest (LAO 1)
J. Michael Francis

Invading Guatemala: Spanish, Nahua,
and Maya Accounts of the Conquest Wars (LAO 2)
Matthew Restall and Florine G. L. Asselbergs

The Conquest on Trial: Carvajal's "Complaint
of the Indians in the Court of Death" (LAO 3)
Carlos A. Jáuregui

Defending the Conquest: Bernardo
de Vargas Machuca's "Apologetic Discourses" (LAO 4)
Edited by Kris Lane and Translated by Timothy F. Johnson

Forgotten Franciscans: Writings from an Inquisitional Theorist,
a Heretic, and an Inquisitional Deputy (LAO 5)
Martin Austin Nesvig